THE SOUNDTRACK OF MY *Life*

SUSAN MARY PAIGE

ISBN 978-1-68526-601-1 (Paperback)
ISBN 978-1-68526-602-8 (Digital)

Copyright © 2022 Susan Mary Paige
All rights reserved
First Edition

All rights reserved. No part of this publication may be reproduced, distributed, or transmitted in any form or by any means, including photocopying, recording, or other electronic or mechanical methods without the prior written permission of the publisher. For permission requests, solicit the publisher via the address below.

Covenant Books
11661 Hwy 707
Murrells Inlet, SC 29576
www.covenantbooks.com

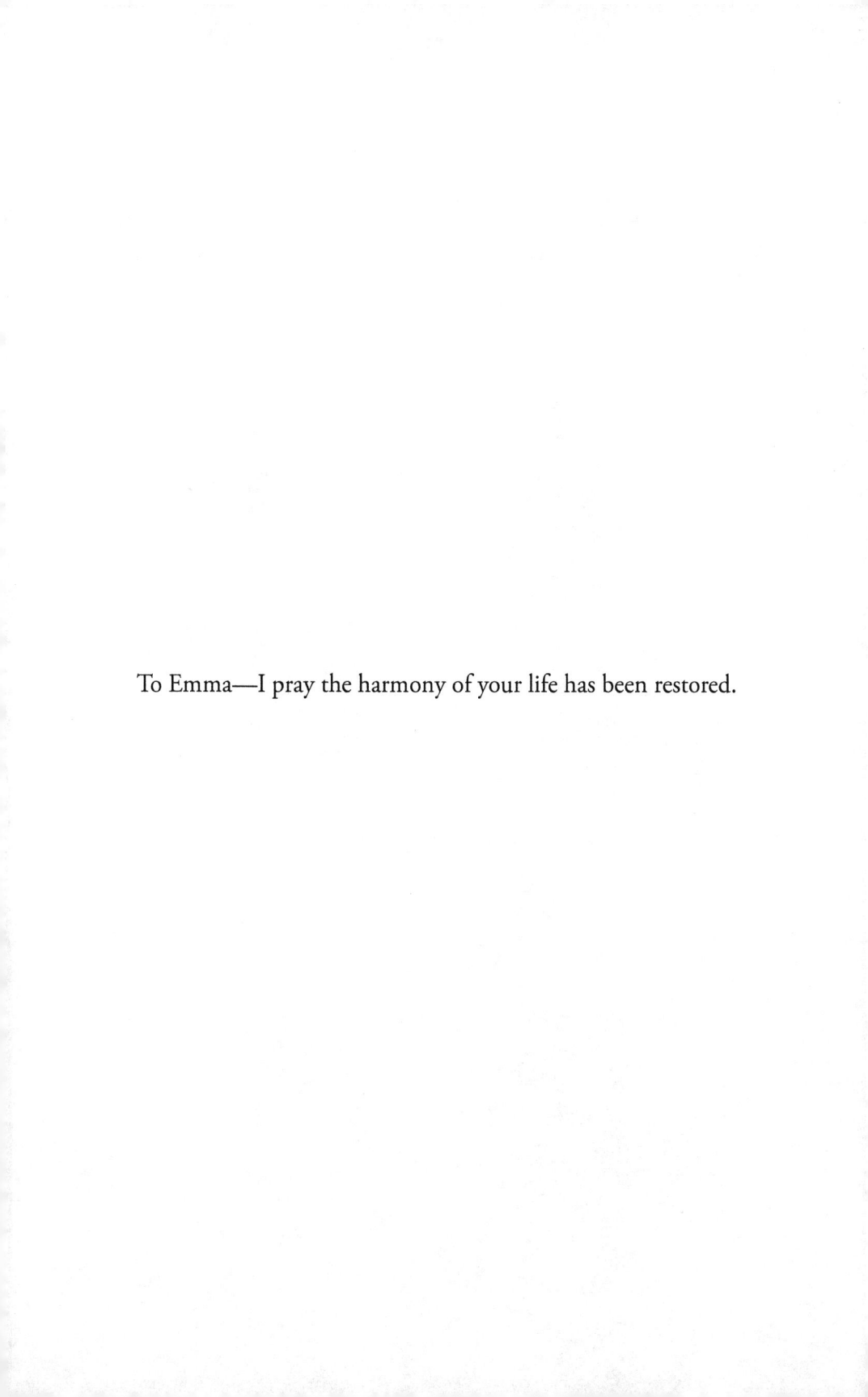

To Emma—I pray the harmony of your life has been restored.

Instead of speaking saintly words we must act them.

—Saint Jerome

Contents

Chapter 1: Introduction 1
Chapter 2: Memories 6
Chapter 3: Helter Skelter 13
Chapter 4: Girl 21
Chapter 5: San Antonio Rose 30
Chapter 6: Yankee Doodle Dandy 37
Chapter 7: It's Raining Men 43
Chapter 8: Annie's Song 51
Chapter 9: Amazing Grace 57
Chapter 10: Speak Softly, Love 63
Chapter 11: Son of a Preacher Man 69
Chapter 12: Mr. Big Stuff 74
Chapter 13: Anticipation 82
Chapter 14: I'm Sorry 87
Chapter 15: My Eyes Adored You 92
Chapter 16: Hey, You Get Off of My Cloud 98
Chapter 17: Somewhere my love 105
Chapter 18: Is that All There Is? 114
Chapter 19: Anticipation: Part 2 120
Chapter 20: We Are the Champions 126
Chapter 21: Oh, the Blooming Bloody Spider 131
Chapter 22: God Bless the USA 139
Chapter 23: The River of Dreams 142
Chapter 24: As Time Goes By 147
Chapter 25: In My Life 155
Chapter 26: One of Us 162
Chapter 27: Life Is a Highway 168
Chapter 28: We Are the Champions: Part 2 174
Chapter 29: We Are Family 183
Chapter 30: Epilogue: Rhythm of the Rain 191

Chapter 1

INTRODUCTION

When you just give love
And never get love
You'd better let love depart
I know it's so, and yet I know
I can't get you out of my heart
You made me leave my happy home
You took my love and now you're gone
Since I fell for you
(Since I Fell for You, Buddy Johnson [1945])

Let me begin this memoir with an explanation of the title—*The Soundtrack of My Life*. You will observe that there is a song lyric at the beginning of this introduction and at the beginning of each chapter. I love music, and it seemed to me a theme emerged as I was writing each chapter, hence the notion of a soundtrack. The lyric I selected for this introduction is from my all-time favorite piece of music; yes, I do love the Beatles, and they have several in the number 2 spot but not here. "If I Fell For You" was written in 1945 but was not a hit in America until 1963—the year of the Beatles invasion. I love the blues genre of music, and no, I am not chronically depressed. All music taps into our deeper self, but the blues go deeper to the heart and soul, and this song is, dare I say, haunting.

Read the first two lines of the lyric. Though these lines are brief, they are, at the same time, somewhat autobiographical. Love is a risky business, and every time, we open ourselves up to it, there is a risk it will not be reciprocated, or it will be betrayed, and/or it will just end badly; on that note, I have had my share of experience. So why do we do it? I believe the reasons are varied, but there seems to be something in us, humans, that needs and wants love—warts and all. By the way, I am not limiting this to romantic love (*eros*). It can also be love for friends (*philos*), the pure giving love that the Creator gives to His creatures (*agape*), and the love and duty of community and culture (*storge*). I discovered a bit of all these love types in writing this memoir in myself and in those I came to know, both living and dead.

I had some very powerful experiences in doing genealogical research on my family. As a Roman Catholic, I was not involved in séances. However, I was able to gather enough information about those who went before me to develop a deeper sense of who they were because part of them resided in me. Because I believe in the communion of saints, I also know that a real connection does exist. My experiences became so powerful that I had to write, and write I have.

As I wrote, I did wonder if this account is an exercise in vanity. Will anyone but me read this? Does anyone but me even care about this story? This whole project seems to be someone else's project, and *they* have constrained me to be their typist. That being written, I must also be clear that this memoir is not automatic writing where some disembodied spirit makes my fingers move to type words. I am a two-finger typist, and any spirit worth their haunting would have me using all ten of my fingers. That adds another level of insanity to this project because I am a terrible typist; I am using two well-worn fingers at this very moment. And yet I continue to type the thoughts and impressions that occur to me. Finally, and maybe more importantly, I am too busy to find myself involved in such egotism, and yet I continue to type.

I have heard several of my favorite authors, and I do not put myself in their talented peer group, say that some of their stories were dictated to them. They had a particular story idea, and they wrote having no idea where the story was going let alone how it was going to end. My dear friend Jane, who teaches college writing, would not approve of this process, *sans* outline and multiple revisions. However, neither of these writers followed Jane's prescription all the time, and they followed this writing process only after they had an established reputation. They, unlike me, are very successful and very rich, so my writing carries a certain level of risk because I possess neither of these characteristics.

Another point of view contends that journaling is accepted to work through personal issues, organize thinking, and plan. I will admit there is some of this self-discovery going on here, and as the story unfolds, that will become apparent. I had a passing curiosity about my genealogy, but it was a cigar box and a dream about my dead paternal grandmother—who I never met—that really got the ball rolling.

This then leads me to another perspective that I need to clarify. Some of you may have a belief in and/or go to mediums who "purportedly mediate communication between spirits of the dead and living human beings" (Wikipedia). I personally reject this practice. Those of you who adhere to this belief will find I agree with your worldview that this physical life is not all there is to our existence. Unlike atheists, I do not believe that we are a mass of tissues and synapses, and it all ends with death. Agnostics will have some agreement with me because you are not sure how it all works, so you are open to possibilities. As a practicing Roman Catholic, I believe in the *communion of saints* (the spiritual union of the members of the Christian Church, living and dead, those on earth, in Heaven, and in Purgatory). This clarification is nothing more than a way to set the stage for this story because my actions and thinking are framed by this perspective.

Beyond my spiritual convictions about contacting the dead, I have some practical considerations. I am muddled enough in this plane of existence and do not need intrusions from the ether to further confuse my state of mind. I am of the age where I begin to wonder if my words and behavior are being analyzed by my children to assess my readiness for the Sunny View Rest Home with their own version of Nurse Ratched. Why would a thoughtful entity from another dimension want to risk putting me in Sunny View? I view that as silencing, if not killing me, the messenger. You might view everything I present in this tome as the babblings of a baby boomer on the verge of senility, but even this has the potential to reveal truths.

So you see my dilemma? On one hand, I am this very busy professional woman who is currently trying to stay under the radar of Sunny View and my children. I am a practicing Catholic Christian. I have a job. I have a great deal to keep me busy, and yet I am still typing this manuscript/journal. I do not go off to mediums to see what spirit is in the room with me and/or to find out what they want me to know. By the way, this too is practical as well as personal because I do believe ignorance is truly bliss. I, for one, do not want to know what is in my future—let alone from people who were just as irrational and misguided as I am on this plane of existence (see Samuel 28:3–25). All of that being written, I am still typing with my two fingers, so I best try to get to the end of this project so I can get the rest of my work done. You should also know that as I write this introduction, the first three chapters are done. Hindsight, as they say, is twenty-twenty, so I have some perspective on the content to follow, *but* I have no idea how this will all end.

In chapter 2, I write about the beginning of this journey, and I use the lyrics from the song, "The Way We Were"—really the refrain "Memories." In writing this chapter, I discovered I could have memories about someone I did not know on this plane of existence without a séance. As the lyric asks, "Can it be that it was all so simple then? Or has time rewritten every line? What's too painful to remember, we simply choose to forget…" It was not until later that the irony in the selection of this lyric became apparent to me. I really thought that what I wrote in chapter 2 was the whole story. I even submitted it for publication as a short story, but no one "found it appropriate for their publication." These rejections (yes, there was more than one) add to my "Why am I doing this?" list of reasons, and yet my two fingers are still typing.

THE SOUNDTRACK OF MY LIFE

I do get to the Beatles in the chapter 3 lyric, "Helter Skelter." This lyric is nowhere in the running for my Beatles's favorite; it is the term "Helter Skelter" that summarizes how I felt while I was making the discoveries I write about in chapter 3. There is a definite change in my tone as I transition. Chapter 2 ends in a peaceful fade to black with the lyric of "The Way We Were" gently drifting on the background. In chapter 3, I am slowly becoming frantic trying to piece together the information I have as I try to make it fit into the reality I thought I knew. The somewhat amusing irregularities in my father's "memories" in chapter 2 become the source of frustration, confusion, and impatience in chapter 3. "Helter Skelter" captures the essence of it perfectly.

Chapter 4 opens with "Girl, You'll Be a Woman Soon" written and performed by Neil Diamond (although there have been many covers for this lyric). The content of this chapter will reveal the appropriateness of this selection, so I will let chapter 4 speak for itself. I will simply write that in chapter 4, my memoir takes a very bewildering turn. I am humbled as I remember my simplistic, and somewhat superior, tone in chapter 2. Everything I thought I knew in chapter 2 begins to unravel in chapter 3 and is turned on its head in chapter 4. Now on the surface, I am hoping to pique your curiosity by not divulging more details, but that is only part of the truth. The reality is that I simply cannot capture the essence of this chapter and do it justice in this small space.

It is interesting to me how this narrative has evolved. My limited literary sense tells me—and yes maybe *someone* else—that this was the best way to construct this story-including writing the introduction (Chapter 1) after chapters 2, 3, and 4 were written. I can take no credit for prescience or cleverness in this approach. Like the rest of the story, it seemed to me that this was what came next. So I hope that if there is someone out there reading this that you will stay with me, and we will both discover how this is going to end because, as of this date, I honestly have no idea.

(In the early chapters, dates were not used to reflect the years I was writing. Eventually, I realized, as the manuscript grew, that some marker dates were helpful.)

Chapter 2

MEMORIES

> Memories, light the corners of my mind
> Misty watercolor memories of the way we were.
> Scattered pictures of the smiles we left behind
> smiles we give to one another
> for the way we were.
> Can it be that it was all so simple then
> or has time rewritten every line?

These lyrics are from Barbara Streisand's classic song, "The Way We Were"; however, I think of the title as "Memories." As I thought about writing this piece, these lyrics, dare I say poem, were very much part of my thinking. This is a paradox in that this piece will focus on death and the resting place of those we have known and those we have not. Specifically, those whose names are just that—a name on a genealogy chart. They are a part of who I am, but what part and how much? Would I like them if we met? Has someone told me I would not? Is that true? Beyond that, what respect do we, the living, owe to them?

For those we have known in a lifetime can and does rewrite every line especially after their passing. If we were predisposed to like them, I suspect we tend to remember the good about them and let the bad pass away. A similar pattern would exist for those of whom we were not particularly fond. However, there is the caveat, "Do not speak ill of the dead." It seems our custom, in general, is to remember the good and allow the other thoughts to pass away whenever possible. Perhaps the belief in another existence beyond this one plants the thought that the dead now know their shortcomings, and our angst will be of no effect.

So why are my musings going to this place? First, I am of an age that such thoughts reflect a coming reality for myself and others I know and love of my age. Second, my family was very cognizant of respecting the dead, and so Memorial Day finds me doing the family task of weeding, cutting, and planting at family graves—wondering all the while if anyone will do the same for me. Third, half of my family knowledge is missing. My father's Philadelphia family is a mystery. I soon learned that some of the meager details I had were not even true—a bleak task indeed.

My father said little to us about his Philadelphia family and most of it was reluctantly. His mother's maiden name was O'Hara, and she died when he was young. He was placed in foster care at age seven. He had an older sister named Nancy. My two brothers and I knew my mother's family, and she exhibited no desire to know her "in-laws." Growing up, we did not feel the loss. Now my mother and her family are gone, and I have first cousins, but I realized that beyond her siblings and their families, I do not know very much. Suddenly, my attention was focused on those who carried the same family name and, aside from my two brothers and their families, I knew nothing about.

My father has been deceased for over thirty years, and I inherited his cigar box filled with pictures that were not marked, World War II memorabilia, a Philadelphia Lodge 2 Elk's club handbook from 1920, a small cameo pendant, and an original Pennsylvania birth certificate for an Aunt Anne, younger than my father, I never knew I had. This is where I began this journey looking for people from another place and perhaps already dead. I had memories but only from my imagination. I had pictures, but who were they? Did I mention that the maiden name of my grandmother, on my aunt's birth certificate, was not the name my father told me? I would get out the cigar box to look at pictures; my frustration would build, and I would put the box away for a time.

My first step was to sort the fifty or so black-and-white 2" x 3" pictures. Those from my father's army career were put in one pile. There were pictures of my father as a young boy in Philadelphia (I knew that because recognized him, I think), and they went into a different pile. The third pile was of folks I did not know, and based on their clothing, they were from the 1930s and 1940s. My father's handwriting, on the back of one picture, declared, "The whole dam family" and no more. More frustration and I put the box away yet again.

Then I had a dream, over twenty years ago, a very vivid dream that seemed like it happened last night. It was twilight, and I was in a cemetery. No horror movie things here; it was serene and peaceful. It was spring or summer; everything was green and lush. A dark-haired woman in a white dress stood before me. The dress was from the early 1900s. It was full-length, high collar, and long sleeved; and she appeared to be in her late twenties. I just knew she was Emma, my father's mother, and she spoke to me. She raised her right arm and pointed off to a mausoleum-like structure and told me it was my job to bring the family together.

She said no more. Did she mean that people were scattered in different burial places? Was my task to literally have graves moved? Was I to track down family members and see them entombed together? Despite the twenty years, this dream has kept me on the path to discovery. Did one of my memories finally have a face? Not really. Emma's features were vague and not in the sharp focus of the surroundings.

My next thought was that I should send for my father's military records. I sent the request and took special care not to tell my mother what I was doing. I waited almost a year for a response—thinking that they would never arrive—and when they did arrive, it took a moment to sink in what I had. Now the conditions of the copies were also a marvel to me. There was a fire at the military storage facility, and the copies showed edges that were singed and burned. I was fortunate to have them. They confirmed the Philadelphia enlist-

THE SOUNDTRACK OF MY LIFE

ment, my grandfather and grandmother's name (still Emma but not O'Hara), and my Aunt Anne's existence. Dad knew he had a sister Anne and said nothing? My father went into the army with one middle name and left with a different one; what was that about? I was still creating memories from my imagination.

My next thought was finding a death notice for my grandfather. My mother told me he died shortly before they were married, and she did not go to the funeral. I wrote to the Philadelphia newspaper of record of the year and requested an archive search for my Pappy's obituary. I now referred to him as Pappy, not grandpa or granddad; he was Pappy. They found nothing.

Dad said he was a big deal in the Elks Club; the booklet in the cigar box must be his, and so I thought the newspaper would have an obituary write-up, and it did not. The Philadelphia Elk's might have records, but the lodge was long gone, and there seemed to be no one to contact. The funeral home was still open in Philadelphia, but my requests for information were never answered. By now, I was getting internet savvy, and I found the vital records for Philadelphia and sent for Pappy's death certificate, but as in all good mysteries, it left me with more questions.

What I learned was that Pappy was older than I expected when my father was born. My math skills served me well. He was sixty-nine when he died, and my dad was twenty-five, so he was forty-four when my father was born—much older than I thought. I went right to the cigar box, and I had his picture. My dad had similar features, and because I knew he was older, I just knew it was Pappy, and I had another face to add to my memories. However, his death certificate listed his parents' names as unknown. Darn! He was from Vermont? What? I was happy of course, but now, I had more questions to search out. I put the box away again.

About ten years ago, I was searching on the internet, and I discovered that Elk's clubs often had an "Elk Rest" section in some cemeteries. What about Philadelphia? Yes, it did; Mount Moriah Cemetery (MMC) was one of the oldest Victorian garden cemeteries in the country. I wrote a letter and received a reply that Pappy was buried there, and it gave me the lot and section number. I could not believe it. How soon could I make the trip? Was my grandmother buried there? I wrote to MMC again and never received a response to my inquiries about my grandmother. In the meantime, I was finishing a PhD, my job was changing, and I was developing mobility problem from childhood polio. The cigar box was put away again.

My grandmother had neither birth nor death records nor could I find a record of her marriage to Pappy. Seeing he was older, was Emma his second wife? My dear friend Gillian has traced her family back many generations, and she was using her memberships to genealogy sites to assist me in looking for family information, and she came up with nothing. I put the cigar box away again.

Then on Saint Patrick's Day in 2010, I was thinking about my father; remember, he told me his mother was an O'Hara from County Cork. He loved the day and dressed in green down to his underwear because of his Irish mother. I thought of Aunt Anne. (Did I mention that as a Roman Catholic, we take a name for our confirmation? When I was thirteen years old, many years ago, I took the name Anne. Even though the spelling is odd, it was identical to my confirmation name.) I did an internet search, and I found an army military record for that name from Philadelphia with the same birth date but a one-year difference; I think she lied about her age to get into the Women's Army Corps. Why not the army? Dad was in the army. Unfortunately, as I followed up, I learned her records were lost in the same fire that almost claimed my dad's. I was able to get her final pay record. She mustered out to Philadelphia, but then she disappeared.

Finally, in the late winter of 2013, a friend wanted to take a summer trip. We had talked about Maine, but then she said south. I have long wanted to go to Gettysburg. Then I could get to MMC. I looked up MMC on the internet and found out it had been abandoned for several years and finally had been taken over by a group of family members who had relatives buried in MMC and were forming a not-for-profit restoration group. Wisely, in hindsight, I wrote to them and connected with Rob. He is a volunteer with over 120 family members buried in the 140 acres of MMC. We exchanged numerous emails, and he was astonished that I ever received a response from MMC when I wrote in 2003. The words he used to refer to the former MMC association were less than charitable, and I again realized how "luck" had been on my side. In addition, my Pappy's grave had been covered in three to four feet of overgrowth until May of 2013 when a volunteer group came to clear the site.

Can you believe that after all of this I was not sure I was up to the drive into Philadelphia? We were staying in Lancaster, and the Philadelphia traffic was murder. My friend Joan and I were dazed by the route, but we finally got there, and Rob and I met face-to-face. My friend was overwhelmed by the size of MMC, the many sites still buried by brush, and the great deal of work the friends of MMC had to do. I was prepared for that because Rob had been sending pictures.

When we got to the site, I knew I was meant to be there. It had been sixty-plus years since Pappy's funeral, and as far as I know since any family had been to the site. It was a lovely spot on the side of a hill. I had made an artificial flower arrangement with Pappy's name on it, hoping maybe someone else might see it and ask questions. Rob was pretty sure there had once been a headstone, but he speculated it had been removed to put in someone else's stone. It was never returned because no one had paid for perpetual care. Because of the miraculous letter, we could identify the exact location of his grave.

It was a mystical moment for me. I *saw* my dad standing at the graveside on a cold March day as his father was being buried. He was ambivalent about the father for whom he had so many mixed feelings. Yet he was still feeling the loss of his father, and this confused and angered him. I know exactly how that felt because I had a similar feeling about family members. In addition, the location looked very much like the location of my dream: it was lush and green and had only weeks before been covered in weeds. An even bigger miracle was that this was an August day in Philadelphia, and the temperature was seventy-one, low humidity, and a soft breeze.

My friend Joan was overwhelmed by the experience. Rob had given us a brief tour of the two sides of MMC—half in Philadelphia County and half in Delaware County. Pappy is on the Delaware side. We saw a Civil War site, and Joan was captivated by MMC. Driving into Philadelphia, she was asking me, "Why are you doing this?" Driving home, she was asking when I would go back.

I now have memories with faces, names, and locations. I was not there when Pappy died and was buried, and I have much more to discover about my family. This trip, dare I say pilgrimage, was an important part of my journey. I knew Pappy was not perfect, but the respect I came to show him was as important for me personally as it was to respect his memory. Some of my success and strength come from him. I did not see this part of the journey before I arrived at MMC, but I see it more clearly now; thanks to another dear friend who told me to write the experience down.

I had the cigar box with me at MMC, and standing there with Pappy's picture in hand let me know I was somewhat closer to my grandmother's request. We were getting closer together at long last, and it had nothing to do with moving graves and everything to do with memories being constructed to light the corners of my mind.

Chapter 3

HELTER SKELTER

When I get to the bottom I go back to the top
    of the slide
Where I stop and I turn and I go for a ride
Till I get to the bottom and I see you again.
When I get to the bottom I go back to the top
    of the slide
And I stop and I turn and I go for a ride
And I get to the bottom and I see you again
Yeah yeah yeah
Look out helter skelter
She's coming down fast.
Yes she is.
Yes she is
(Helter Skelter, *White Album;* The Beatles
    [1968])

I wanted to call this segment part 2 of my family Odyssey, but it is an indication of a lesson learned since I last wrote that I had best call it chapter 3. As I returned from my trip to Philadelphia, I was filled with assurance that I had deciphered my grandmother Emma's cryptic message from beyond the grave to "bring the family together." At the time, I was relieved that I was not literally moving graves into the same geographic location but rather just collecting memories so that family members will not be forgotten.

Now, two years later, the court orders and cemetery plots seem such a simple task compared to the tangle I have uncovered and hence the reference to "Helter Skelter." I should add here that I selected this musical element as much for the instrumentation as the lyric. Listen to the music. It is dissonant, loud, and unsettling just like my family discoveries.

Let me begin with my knowledge of Pappy (my paternal grandfather). With the help of Gillian, a good friend who is very good at things genealogical, I began to untangle the confusion. I think of where Pappy was born and when. Timothy Paige (1819–1884) and Rebecca Richardson had multiple children including two sons named George and Edwin. George married a woman named Louisa (no last name available) and had a male child born on November 4, 1884, also no name on the birth record. Edwin married Ella Hill and had a son Frank Hill Paige born on September 29, 1878. It appears that both male children were born in Proctorville, Vermont. The confusion arose because Pappy's death certificate list his DOB as November 4, 1878.

A subsequent draft record for Frank Albert Paige dated September 12, 1918, lists a DOB of November 4, 1884, and a father's name as George. I believe, as much as I can be sure in these matters, my paternal grandfather is the son born to George and Louisa (Blanchard) Paige of Proctorville, Vermont, on November 4, 1884, and that Frank Hill Paige was his first cousin born to Pappy's uncle Edwin in 1878. This sounds so much simpler as I am writing this, but it was months of reflection on my part to untangle it all. I have yet to discover why the dates were confused on Pappy's death certificate. It appears my father provided the information so only God knows what Dad knew about the facts and, considering that his other genealogical information was less than reliable, the errors seem perfectly reasonable.

There was a silver lining to all this, however. It seems that Timothy Paige was a direct descendant of Col. Timothy Paige (1727–

1791) of the Revolutionary Army of the Republic and a member of the Committee of Correspondence.

> Shadow governments organized by the Patriot leaders of the Thirteen Colonies on the eve of the American Revolution…The committees became the leaders of the American resistance to British actions, and largely determined the war effort at the state and local level. (wikipedia.com)

This makes your humble author eligible to join the Daughters of the American Revolution (DAR). The Paige line seemed very straightforward, and I can tell you I never saw that coming.

It appears the Paige family was a big deal in Proctorville, Vermont, and they were all involved, in one way or another, in the wool trade. Pappy, unlike his cousin Frank Hill Paige, was not interested in the family business and somehow got to Akron, Ohio, and then Philadelphia, Pennsylvania, but again, only God knows how, sounds like material for subsequent chapters. However, this discovery of a very WASP (White, Anglo-Saxon Protestant) lineage on the Paige side makes my father's marriage to a second-generation Catholic, Polish-American woman would not be thought of too highly.

I support this conclusion with three vignettes that tend to support my assessment of my Paige ancestors. One was a remark made by a friend who was from Philadelphia and born in the early twentieth century. I showed her some of the pictures in the cigar box, several of which I believe contained Pappy, and she commented, "I can tell you one thing: these people had money. I can tell how they are dressed." My father always said Pappy had money, but he lost it before he died in 1947.

The second was a story my mother always told about her first date with my father: he took her to the opera *Aida*, and it was not even in English. At the time, that statement meant little to me, but as my own cultural awareness expanded, I realized that most post-World War II vets from South Philly were not flooding Opera Houses. First dates, then and now, are about making a good first impression, and my mother was not as much impressed as she was bemused and uncomfortable on her first date with my father. Opera is an acquired taste, and my father's view of making a good impression was very different from my mother's.

Third was my father loved boating, and as the family relocated to the shores of Lake Erie, on the Great Lakes where my mother's family lived, he had a boat, and he joined the yacht club. Now he had a twenty-seven-foot powerboat, not a yacht by any standards, but when my parents traveled on the Great Lakes in the boat, they could stay at other yacht clubs. My mother was very uncomfortable around wealthy people, and she often complained that my dad was right at home with them. He struck up conversations and lingered when she wanted to run away. I think it is reasonable to conclude my father came from money old money in fact. This being true, I am sure several of my WASP Paige ancestors were rotating in their graves when my father married this working-class Polish Catholic girl from upstate New York. You know, now that I think of it, that might have been his point.

During this time, I also found some information about my Aunt Anne. She was married to a man named Owen and died in Philadelphia in May of 1988. Try as I may, I keep hitting a dead end with her. Her death certificate listed her occupation as an accountant for a supermarket chain. For those of you who are old enough to remember, there was a supermarket chain called Anne Page, and my younger brother and I used to joke we could be part of this and not know it; now, I really wonder. By the way, Aunt Anne's death certificate listed her mother's information as unknown.

So this brings me to Emma—literally the apparition in my dream—who asked me to bring the family together. Oh my goodness, what a request this has become! Anne was five years old when Emma died, and I find it striking that her mother's name was unknown to the informants who provided the information for her death certificate. We are asked for our mother's maiden name so often I find it curious that her father's name, my Pappy, is listed but Emma is not.

At this point, I should add that I had been working on an online genealogy for more than seven years. As I unearthed information, I would add it to the chart just to help me keep the information sorted *and* in a fond hope that someone was looking for Pappy's offspring like me. As I wrote earlier, I was not about to pay for access to data that should be public information, and I had friends, like Gillian, who helped me track down the family. Every so often, the sites do offer free access, and the Fourth of July, 2015, weekend was such an occasion. It was the day that everything I thought I knew changed.

As was my usual practice, I began searching for Aunt Anne, and as usual, I hit a dead end. Next, I typed in Emma's name, and I had a hit on the motherlode of all good genealogical information: her death certificate. I was sure it was another Emma, but the first thing I saw was her husband's name: it was Pappy. Her parents' names were listed, and my entire lifelong belief in my Irish ancestry vanished in the blink of an eye. My great-grandmother's name was Lysel—Pennsylvania Dutch if am I correct. If that was all there was, I would have found this information very revealing and astonishing but it was not.

Emma died in Philadelphia on January 16, 1929; there was a coroner's inquest on January 17, 1929, and she was buried in Harrisburg, Pennsylvania on January 18, 1929. A coroner's inquest? How did she die? Harrisburg? Why such a fast burial? While I was reading this, I had one of those moments that I will always remember where I was and what I was doing because I was not expecting what came next. My grandmother's cause of death was from "septicemia from an incomplete abortion—probably self-inflicted." I read and reread and then asked my cousin to read it to make sure I had not made a mistake.

Suddenly, so many blocks of information fell into place; it was like an emotional avalanche. No wonder my father was confused about names. (When I got a copy of my father's death certificate, my mother had listed his mother's name as Nancy O'Hara.) Grandma Emma was from Harrisburg, Pennsylvania, and I would learn more about this later. Her parents took her home quickly for burial, and I know that any relationship between Emma's family and Pappy was over. Dad was almost seven when she died but still young enough that the repetition of his "new" family history would become the truth for him. O'Hara? Why not? It is as good a last name as any. Most folks in the twenty-first century would not discuss this type of death, but in 1929, it had to be beyond anyone's ability to comprehend. So for Emma's family, they proceeded with "we forget about Emma, forget about Pappy and Dad, and, worst of all, never mention Emma again, and it will go away." Life goes on.

Emma was almost forty, and Pappy was forty-four years old when she died. They had two children ages six and four. How did they meet? Why did they marry? What was the condition of their marriage? For whatever reason, Emma was so desperate that she sought to terminate her pregnancy. I think the "probably self-inflicted" was added to the cause of death because anything else would require law enforcement involvement. The hope here was to settle matters in Philadelphia, bury her quickly in Harrisburg, and try to forget the whole awful events. It meant Emma's parents cut their relationship with their grandchildren, my dad and Anne, but they also cut their relationship with Pappy. I am sure there was more than enough blame to go around again and again and again.

My dad was put in a foster home after Emma died, and he was always bitter about this because Pappy did not keep him. I learned this information when, as a young adult, I accompanied Dad to an AA (Alcoholics Anonymous) meeting. Dad was an active and well-known AA member in Western New York, and he was often asked to be a guest speaker, stutter and all, at a meeting. The meeting was about forty-five miles away, and Dad asked me to accompany him. Looking back on that opportunity now, I realized it was a seminal moment for me.

Dad told his story and began with his childhood and young adult life stories I had never heard before his death. His relationship with Pappy was very strained. Dad was put in a foster home after Emma died, but he apparently maintained some contact with Pappy. He said Pappy did not consider him much of a man because of the aftereffects of spinal meningitis (premature balding, speech impediment, a classic 120-pound weakling frame, and a twenty-eight-inch waist until he died in 1977) Dad had at age four. Of course, the fact Dad survived this illness in the 1920s is a miracle. Apparently, the high fever left Dad with a stutter, premature balding, and weak eyes; he literally looked like the ninety-eight-pound weakling in the old bodybuilding ad. (Think of the Steve Rogers character in *Captain America* before Howard Stark beefs him up.)

My dad joined the army to prove Pappy wrong. Of course, under no other circumstances would the army ever take him, but it was war time and Dad had a pulse. Dad was a medical corpsman and saw some of the worst action in North Africa and Europe with General Patton. After WWII, he came home to Philadelphia and Pappy. Dad tried to work with Pappy in his nightclub, but that did not work; they just did not get along. He reenlisted in the army, went to Texas, met my mother, and the rest, as they say, is history. I never heard this story told again.

I wrote a letter to Dad's foster family after he died in 1977. I knew that Christmas cards were exchanged every year, and my mother had the address. His foster mother had died, but her daughter Dot wrote to tell me what little she knew about Pappy. (I deeply regret that letter is gone, and I have not been able to find that thread again.) She wrote that Pappy was a gymnast (What!) and used to compete; this could explain his macho attitude toward Dad.

Dad said his father owned a nightclub during the Depression, and he was very well-off financially. In my later years, I realized that the Depression was also during Prohibition and so that meant his nightclub was probably a speakeasy. What are the implications of that? I also remembered Dad used to say the Mafia was not just Italians, and I now really think that his knowledge on these subjects was more than an incidental opinion he heard on a Philadelphia trolley car.

After my father died, I made the mistake of sharing my growing suspicions about Pappy's business connections with my mother. My mother and I were sitting in her living room watching a movie about the mafia. The movie content tripped my thoughts, and in all innocence, I said, "I think Dad's father had connections to the mafia." My mother went ballistic and told me to *never* say such a thing again to *anyone*. *Wow*, what had I tapped into? In spite of the threat, I told my youngest brother and my cousin, and they both responded, "I wonder what she knew?"

I had all this information floating around in my head in random thoughts, but in an instant, when I saw Emma's cause of death, it fell together, and I understood the immense secret everyone was trying to forget. It explained many things, and I thought I had finally discovered what Emma was trying to tell me in the dream. The families were fractured, and if I could reach out to other surviving relatives, I could begin to rebuild connections. Of course, that would make sense based on what I had learned. What happened next made me realize that I had only begun to scratch the surface.

What is the lyric in "Helter Skelter?"

> When I get to the bottom I go back to the top
>   of the slide
> Where I stop and I turn and I go for a ride
> Till I get to the bottom and I see you again.

I realize now there were important questions about Emma and Pappy that I never bothered to ask let alone pursue. For example, their marriage was later in life. Why? I still do not have a great deal of information about those years, but now, I know where to look for the gaps, and I am armed with a whole new set of questions.

Remember the online genealogy chart I wrote about earlier? In January of 2016, I received an email with an inquiry about Emma. Nancy was seeking information about her aunt Edna. Edna was adopted by her mother's older sister and she died in 1981. In looking at the adoption papers, Nancy identified Edna's birth mother as Emma from Harrisburg, Pennsylvania. The minute I read her email, I knew it was true. So what happened to Emma in the years before she married Pappy?

I contacted Nancy. I do not believe Alice's wonderland rabbit hole had the subterranean levels I was about to encounter and wander about. I was going to go deeper into my grandmother's plea—as I was coming to see it—to find out what bringing the family together really meant.

Chapter 4

GIRL

> Girl, you'll be a woman soon
> Please come take my hand
> Girl, you'll be a woman soon
> Soon, you'll need a man
> (Girl, You'll Be a Woman Soon; *Just for You*, Neil
>   Diamond [1967])

Emma was born on August 20, 1889, to John and Lysel, in Harrisburg Pennsylvania. In my laser focus on learning about my Paige ancestors, it never occurred to me to ponder why it was Emma who came in my dream. I suppose I had a fleeting thought about her desire to reunite her family and Pappy's. Even when I saw Emma's death certificate and felt the violent rupture that occurred between the two families, I was still only thinking about Emma as a messenger and, at most, a tragic figure. As I transfer the perspective of this story to Emma, I think of her watching me flounder with all this information; I am glad that her spirit-self could not wield a 2x4.

The other thing that I realized was that I was devaluing Emma's story because she was not a progenitor of the Paige clan. I was looking to the male line to discover more about the name I bear and by extension who I am. In doing this, I ignored my own life experiences. My youngest child, Amanda Irene, not only bears my mother Irene's name but also she is my mother in, oh, so many ways. Amanda's oldest daughter, Olivia, is so much like me; we can easily finish each other's sentences. In neither case is there a physical resemblance; it is rather a like-mindedness that is uncanny.

When my mother died, Amanda and I had to go to my mother's home and find five different pieces of documentation for the funeral director. Within five minutes, while I was considering where to begin, Amanda laid all five documents on the table. All I could say was, "How?" Amanda's response was, "I just thought like Grandma, and I knew where to look." Needless to say, the rest of my mother's funeral arrangement decisions were made by Amanda because I was 95 percent sure Amanda's selections would coincide with her grandmother's wishes.

I should add here that my mother and I had none of that synergy. Interestingly, she would always tell me, usually in an exasperated tone, that I was "…just like your father!" And she did not mean it as a compliment. Perhaps my mother's statement programmed me to think of myself as a Paige, like my dad, but how much of my father's persona reflected Emma? Dad did not know her, so he would be unable to identify that for himself or for me. How often I would say to Amanda, "You are just like your grandmother!" I readily admit that such statements can become self-fulfilling prophecies, but that does not explain how Amanda found those papers. No one in my family could say to me "you are just like your Grandma Emma!" because no one knew anything about Emma until I received the email from Nancy.

When Nancy and I began to communicate, I had no idea where this would lead. Nancy's family named my aunt Edna, but she was not adopted until she was about a year old, and she was called Ruth before this. Nancy and I referred to her as Edna/Ruth. I saw Edna/Ruth as another branch, though a surprising one, on my ever-growing family tree; she was my aunt after all. We wanted to be sure that the Emma, who was the birth mother of her aunt, was the same Emma that was my grandmother. As I have indicated previously, Emma was older, thirty-three and thirty-five respectively, when she gave birth to Dad and Anne. Prior to Nancy's contact, I had discovered proof that Pappy was not Emma's first husband. In July of 1914, at the age of twenty-four, the marriage license indicates twenty-two, Emma had married Charles in Harrisburg, Pennsylvania. This news was not a surprise, and in fact, it helped me make more sense out of Emma having my father in her thirties. In the twenty-first century, this is very common, but in the early twentieth century, a woman was often considered an "old maid" if she was unmarried at age twenty-five.

In looking at the records of Emma's marriage to Charles, I noticed that in the 1914 document, Emma's birth date was listed at 1892, not 1889, and Charles was listed as 1892. (It is clearly my Emma because her parents are listed as Lysel and John.) This lends proof to the supposition made above about the expiration date on women in the early 1900s. Three years, even three years older than her husband is no big deal in the twenty-first century, but in 1914, it did make a difference. Was Emma, after the birth of Edna/Ruth, the blushing rose or the decorative greenery in the bouquet of young maidens in Harrisburg? I am not one to determine female worth based on dress size and glamour, so at first glance, I thought little about this fact.

There were several anomalies with Charles, however. In a 1900 census of Charles' family, he is listed as age six, meaning he was born in 1894. Now it appears that Charles's age was increased, and Emma's age was decreased to make them both twenty-two years old at their July 1914 wedding. Again, if Emma was lower on the desirability scale, I guess I can see the need to cast about to make a respectable marriage, but this change begins to have a feel of coercion to it.

Then I received Nancy's email asking if her aunt Edna could be the child of my grandmother Emma. Edna was born on April 25, 1912—a little more than a year before Emma's marriage to Charles. Yes, this would work on the calendar, but more importantly, I knew it was true; perhaps I was sensing an ethereal 2x4 in the vicinity. Edna was born Ruth May to Emma and an unknown father, and the petition for adoption was approved on March 23, 1914—two and a half months before Emma's marriage to Charles. This would make her my aunt as well and my father's half-sister, so Nancy and I now refer to her as Aunt Edna/Ruth. Our aunt died on March 12, 1981.

Another question you may be asking is how did Nancy's grandparents come to adopt Emma's child? Nancy's great-grandmother was a very close friend of Lysel. In addition, Nancy's great-grandfather worked on the Pennsylvania Railroad with my Grandfather John, Emma's father. We wondered if Edna Ruth went to her adoptive parents immediately after birth. Nancy wrote,

> I too have speculated as to whether or not Edna/Ruth went to my grandparents at birth; I am wondering if it was a matter of two friends, Catherine and Lysel, making this plan while Emma was pregnant. I say that because my grandmother had lost two babies and was apparently told she would not be able to have children. She had two miscarriages and was told that she probably could not have children. (Personal Communication; February 2015)

I realized that Edna/Ruth was with her birth family for some time before the adoption. They named her Ruth May, and she is referred to by that name in the adoption petition that requested that she now be known as Edna. After Nancy's Grandmother Edith adopted Edna/Ruth, Edith went on to have four children of her own. Nancy's mother is the youngest of these four children.

When Nancy and I began this correspondence, there was an unintended consequence that was quite wonderful: I had personal information on a blood relative of my father. Could I begin to see a family resemblance? If so, we can attribute it to Emma because she was the common denominator: she is the mother of Edna/Ruth and my dad. Here is Nancy's description of Edna:

> Edna graduated with honors from John Harris High School and became an RN. I have a picture of her graduating class from Harrisburg Hospital's School of Nursing. She was a permanent fixture in our home, more like a doting

grandmother than an aunt. She spent her last years in our home. She never married, and I never heard of any romantic attachments on her part. She was not like us at all. We are a family of tall thin people; Edna was petite with the most delicate feet and hands. She loved baseball, game shows, and, in better days, traveling to the Jersey *Shore* with friends. She made a trip to Nova Scotia. Edna loved Christmas, made sure we had a generous supply of gifts, gave us allowances weekly, took us shopping for school shoes and for haircuts. She sang Christmas carols, often in Latin, and had a terrible voice.

My father was a small built man. He was about five feet six inches, and he had a twenty-eight inch waist until the day he died. He was a medical corpsman in the army and wanted to get his RN but did not reach that goal. My dad *loved* Christmas and the New York Yankees. He went to the Jersey shore as a boy; he spoke of it often, and he and my mother traveled a great deal, his idea not hers, including Nova Scotia. Nancy concurred with these similarities, and she was pretty sure the Yankees were Edna/Ruth's favorite team. Is there a gene to predispose one to be a Yankee fan?

I want to go back to where I began this chapter. I lamented that there was no way to know what characteristics could be attributed to Pappy or Emma like I could do with Amanda and my mother. When I read Nancy's email, it was like a door opened in a section of my world that had been sealed all my life—so much so that I never even know that the door was there. As the realization dawned on me, I thought I might have heard a gentle sigh of relief off in the distance coming from the soul that visited me in a dream so many years ago. Now she could put down that 2x4.

That was not the end of my learning however. Nancy sent me clippings about Emma as a teenager. She played the piano; I had seen census data from 1920 that listed her occupation as a pianist. Emma played in church and was a featured soloist at age sixteen.

At age seventeen, it was reported that she accompanied a solo vocal performance at a birthday party. In 1905, 1906, and 1907, she was reported as an attendee in social events in Harrisburg. I do not have a photograph of Emma, but what was beginning to emerge was an image of a very talented and socially adept young woman who spent her adolescence socializing with the better classes of Harrisburg.

I do not see Emma's social life on par with the likes of the Rockefellers and the Andrew Carnegies, but the reporting in the local press is indicative of a higher social standing in the Harrisburg community. She was known, and she was invited, and that established her reputation as a desirable social companion. Nancy told me that Lysel and her family attended the same church as her great-grandmother. The whole lot of them were quite WASP from all appearances. I believe that the data I have would allow me to conclude that Emma was a cultured and respected member of her peer group. In addition, her artistic talent on the piano further indicates her cultural interests. Dare I say Emma presented as a suitable prospect for an advantageous marriage.

Cue in the lyrics for the theme song for this chapter, "Girl, you'll be a woman soon…soon you'll need a man." How old is this story? What happened in June of 1911? (Remember Edna/Ruth was born in March of 1912.) Or should I ask *who* changed Emma's life forever in that fateful June? Was the act that began Edna/Ruth's life an assault? Was it consensual? Was Edna/Ruth's father Emma's soul mate? Was he a cad and a manipulator who seduced Emma? Did he love Emma and want to marry her? Did his family, not seeing Emma as a suitable match, respond with a one-way ticket far away for him and a checkbook for my great grandparents?

As I go on with this search, I hope to find some threads to assist me in asking the right questions so I can get the right answers.

Nancy told me an interesting story about her family lore regarding Edna/Ruth's father.

> Your ideas about Emma and the conception
> of Aunt Edna/Ruth sound very likely. My sisters
> do not have the name of any specific individual

with respect to paternity. Someone once told them that a member of the wealthy family may have been involved.

Do I have any proof? No, I do not, but it has the ring of truth to it. It makes complete sense to me that Emma would want this story told. Even though this is the twenty-first century, some things do not change. (Personal Communication from Nancy)

When a young girl is pregnant and not married, she and her prospects are, at best, ruined and, at least, derailed (I could not resist a railroad metaphor). The man gets a shake of the head and a muttered "Boys will be boys." Whoever was Edna/Ruth's father, he shattered any prospects Emma had for a good marriage. I do not believe Charles was the father of Edna/Ruth nor do I believe he was the husband Emma hoped to have. I mean no slander for Charles, but I just do not think he was the husband Emma dreamed of her whole life as girls want to do. She certainly did not have the ideal wedding either.

The newspaper account of Emma and Charles's marriage, in the *Harrisburg Daily Independent*, was two sentences long. They were married in the office of an alderman, at night, and they were "unattended." One could suppose that they eloped because the notice of their obtaining a marriage license was on page five of the paper, and the notice of their brief nocturnal nuptials was on page three. I believe it is safe to assume that *someone* was in a hurry at any rate. The term "unattended" could mean there were only three individuals present, without even witnesses, or it could mean some mixture of family. Whatever the makeup of the participants, it was not a public celebration, in a church, where Emma seemed to spend so much of her adolescent years.

As the research continued on Charles and his family, the picture grew darker. Emma and Charles were married on July 17, 1913. Within two years, *The Harrisburg Telegraph* of January 1915 lists Charles for (military) desertion and nonsupport. In July of 1916, a divorce suit was filed, and in January of 1918, a divorce was granted to Emma and Charles. The story does not end there, however, because in April of 1922, a notice was posted for a petition to appoint a guardianship of Charles who was "recently adjudged insane." Truth, as they say, is indeed stranger than fiction. Charles was dead in July of 1923. His obituary indicates he was a World War I veteran, and he died in a Washington, DC, government hospital.

In fairness to Charles, it should be noted that World War I was beginning in Europe in the summer of 1913. The United States entered the war after the sinking of the *Lusitania* in May of 1915. Charles was a member of the National Guard in the spring and summer of 1914, but there seemed to be no indication that he had combat experience only that he was part of a troop encampment at Gretna, Pennsylvania. Post-Traumatic Stress Disorder (PTSD) really became a concern for veterans returning from World War I, but there was nothing to indicate Charles was afflicted with PTSD. Mental illness does not emerge one day like the common cold. The evidence mounts that Emma's marriage to Charles was an attempt to solve the offspring problems for these two families.

Somewhere the idea has emerged (if you ask me from Hell) that marriage will settle down and/or create maturity in otherwise troubled individuals. The history of Emma and Charles's marriage is a cautionary tale to advise others that this approach to mental health does not work. I am not certain about Emma's emotional state in the winter of 1918, after her divorce from Charles, but having endured something similar, I think she was fragile. One last fact to throw on the information pile was that Charles's father worked for the Pennsylvania Railroad with my Great Grandpa John and Edna/Ruth's adopted father. Sounds like Emma's difficulties were dealt with through the friends and family plan with no professionals in sight.

A sad epitaph to this sorry affair is that the obituaries of Emma's parents John (1944) and Lysel (1984) never mention Emma as predeceasing them in death. To be denied by one's own family is the deepest cut of all. I am not a raving feminist nor do I support the victim mentality, but Emma's story is a cautionary tale. I suspect she died a very deeply disturbed woman.

In the summer of 1911, her dreams were shattered, and by January of 1929, at age thirty-nine, she lay dying in a Philadelphia hospital of a septic infection. It appears she could not bear another child. (I have named that child Uncle George, by the way, and I believe they are together now.) Emma's death left two young children without a mother. My father, who survived spinal meningitis at age four, was put in a foster home at age seven. His less than masculine features caused his father to reject him. These events all had a direct impact on my life, so these events are personal for me.

I am beginning to understand why it was Emma who came to me. Her direction to "bring the family together" goes so far beyond my first imaginings. I will admit to one thing I have learned up to this point: I do not believe Emma is done with me yet. Emma was divorced in 1918, and Dad was not born until 1922, so what happened during those years?

Chapter 5

SAN ANTONIO ROSE

Deep within my heart
Lies a melody,
A song of old San Antone,
Where in dreams I live
With a memory,
Beneath the stars all alone.
Well, it was there I found
Beside the Alamo
Enchantment strange as the
Blue up above,
For that moonlit pass
That only he would know
Still hears my broken song of love.
(San Antonio Rose, Bob Wills [1938])

I choose to use the lyrics of "San Antonio Rose" as the signature lyric to represent this chapter because it is so relevant to the first part of my life. This song has had several successful recording releases, one of them by Patsy Cline. I was fourteen years old when she died in a plane crash, and I have always loved her music. I was born in San Antonio, Texas, in June of 1948. The rose is not only the flower of my birth month but also it is my favorite flower. My birth took place in Brook Army Hospital, Fort Sam Houston, in San Antonio. My father was a medical corpsman in the army, and my mother had been an army nurse. They met and married at Fort Sam, and both of my parents were far away from their hometowns.

My mother was born and raised in a small town, on the shores of Lake Erie, in upstate New York-Dunkirk. My father was from Philadelphia, Pennsylvania. She was a second-generation Polish-American and the first member of her family to have a post high school education. My father was a high school dropout, but he earned his GED while in the army. My mother was from a close-knit ethnic family, and my father knew no family ties. She was a Democrat to his Republicanism. She was Roman Catholic, and he was personally agnostic, though it seemed his foster family was Jehovah's Witness. She traces back one generation to Poland, and he is from strong WASP/New England roots that go back beyond the American Revolution. In order for my mother to agree to marry him, however, my father converted to Roman Catholicism. My mother and father were like oil and water, and they did not mix well—ever.

I was their firstborn. My brother was born in January of 1950—the same year I contracted the polio virus. I was paralyzed from the waist down at the onset and had to learn to walk again. I did my rebab at Fort Sam with World War II vets who had to learn to walk again because Fort Sam was where the worst cases were sent. My memories from that time were vague but pleasant. I was loved and protected by my "military guard." When I was four years old, my father received orders to go to Europe. My mother, who left the military, was not interested in taking two small children, one with the aftereffects of polio, to Europe, so she took my brother and I to Dunkirk to live with her mother, brothers, and sister.

I want to interject here that if you live long enough, you do see life go full circle. After the onset of my polio, I was on crutches, and I had a leg brace. Eventually, I learned to walk on my own, and after I had corrective surgeries, I was rid of the brace. I spent about fifty years with a slight limp—except when I was tired and then, as my mom would say, I was dragging my left leg. Eventually, my right leg began to fail, muscle pain in particular, and I went first to a cane, and now, I am back on crutches and my trusty scooter, but I digress.

Even though I was only four years old, I did remember getting out of the car when we arrived at Dunkirk; there was snow on the ground. I had never seen snow, and I think I was being warned that snow was, from that point on, an integral part of my environment and my life. I missed my dad terribly in those years. I did dream if he came home to us, my mother would not yell so much, and life would be good. She was drinking in Dunkirk and, as I learned later, he was drinking in Europe. Little did I know, when I was about ten years old and I found him sitting at the kitchen table one morning, he was home for good. It did not take long to realize that the life I envisioned if Dad would just come home was never going to happen; it was just a dream closer to a nightmare.

I hate alcohol—the kind people drink to get drunk. So many folks complain about smoking, but cigarettes and dying of cancer did not kill my family and otherwise create chaos. Alcohol destroyed and/or killed most of my family. My mother's father, an alcoholic, killed himself when she was nine years old. My father's father died a broke alcoholic. My father died, after fifteen years of sobriety, because he began drinking again—dead at fifty-five. My mother blamed her drinking on my dad; she never bothered to look at her own family. My youngest brother Jim was very nearly dead from alcohol and drugs. As my two fingers type this, he is clean and sober today, but tomorrow is yet to come; we have both learned to take it one day at a time. Whenever the family got together, everyone was drinking. Going out with my mother's family, they would stop at a local "gin mill," as they called it, for "just one drink." Hours later, my cousins and I were begging to go home so we could go to bed. And yes, they drove us home; how did I survive?

When my mother was drunk, she was mean, and when my father drank, he was sad and maudlin, so that was another difference between them. My father had seven hospital admissions in eight years for his alcoholism. He found that AA was his road to sanity, and he begged my mother to go to meetings. She refused because she said she did not have a drinking problem because she could go to work and did not drink in the morning. All I will say about that is that by 12:01 p.m., she was consuming her first drink of the day.

Dad always quipped that he was an alcoholic, and she was a drunk because he went to meetings and she did not. When I was in college, I went to meetings with Dad, as I described in a prior chapter, and I learned more about him than what he told us at home—particularly how difficult his relationship with Pappy, my grandfather, was. My mother did quit drinking on her own, but none of us know the story. Needless to say, I do not drink!

During all this chaos, I was being treated for my polio. I had a "dropped left foot," and the muscles in my lower left leg ware atrophied, so I had three corrective surgeries. When I was six years old, they fused my ankle; when I was seven years old, they shortened my Achilles tendon, and when I was twelve years old, they broke my leg in two places to straighten it out. In between all of this were shock treatments to regenerate my muscles (it did not work; it just hurt), swimming (which I loved and still do), and a full summer in a cast from toe to hip to straighten my leg and avoid the third surgery; it did not work. The best thing to come out of this was my neighbor taught me to crochet to keep me from going crazy, and it is still working.

My dad loved education. His drinking delayed his ability to use the GI Bill to get his RN degree. When he did go back to a community college, there was too much water under the bridge, and he only lasted a semester; in fact, I helped him with his writing course. I have a PhD today because my dad always valued and supported my educational goals. It became important to me because it was important to him. I did not go back for my doctoral studies until I was almost fifty years old, and my dad was dead for over twenty years. I dedicated my doctoral dissertation to him.

My professional life advanced smoothly, for the most part, unless it was derailed by problems in my personal life. The empathy I have for my grandmother Emma comes, for the most part, in walking a path like her own. I will not go into many details, just the outcomes: (a) unmarried and pregnant at 20, (b) three marriages one to the male in (a), (c) three divorces, (d) three children—two girls and a son, (e) seven grandchildren. As I write, I cannot help but think about how Emma never lived to see her grandchildren—one of whom is me. Grandchildren are such a delight, and as I remind my children that their children are my reward for raising them.

I suggested at the beginning of this chapter that there should be a different melody for the latter part of my life. I would suggest that I have built a strong case for "Looking for Love in All the Wrong Places" (Wanda Mallette, Bob Morrison, and Patti Ryan [1980]). I love my children dearly and comfort myself with the thought that the children husband 1 and 2 fathered were, by far, the best thing they ever did. Interestingly, my son Jimmie takes after my father in looks, physical build, and sports fanaticism, (i.e., New York Yankees). Little did I know, when I began this memoir, that some of these qualities would show up in my genetic line.

I never saw the physical resemblance between my son and my father. They have temperament issues in common, the Yankees and sports in general being the most notable. (One of my favorite stories about my son was that he learned long division so he could calculate Don Mattingly's batting average after each at bat.) Olivia, my oldest granddaughter, was at my home and said, "Who is in that picture that looks like Uncle Jimmie?" I could not guess what picture she was referring to, so I caught my breath when I realized she was looking at a picture of my dad. I had never seen the resemblance, and I was stunned that it had to be pointed out to me.

What I learned later was that my son had a special link to Dad. Jimmie was born in April of 1976, and Dad died in May of 1977, so he knew my dad as well as a one-year-old child knows anyone. As an adult, Jimmie has been in bands for almost twenty years, and he is always nervous before a performance; he is the lead singer. Before a gig, he used to look at a wedding picture of my parents and have a "conversation" with my dad to calm himself before the show. He told me this when I was telling him about Olivia's observation of the family resemblance between him and my father.

I never knew anything about the connection Jimmie felt with my father. He said he had the "conversation" because he just felt a bond with Dad. I spent a great deal of time regretting that my Dad and Jimmie had not inhabited this mortal plane for more than thirteen months because I imagined them going to Yankee games together. Dad took my brother and I to a Yankee double header in Cleveland. It was me who took Jimmie to Cooperstown and the Baseball Hall of Fame and to his first Yankee game in the Bronx.

Jimmie and I share the belief that we do not go to mediums to contact the dead, although we both have deep spiritual beliefs. Something tells me we had hidden company on those trips. One could argue that because I talked to Jimmie about the characteristics he shared with Dad, I had some influence on his thinking. I should add though that when Jimmie was seven years old, he went to live with his father, and I moved 350 miles away until he was eighteen years old. My contact with him was restricted to holiday and summer visits during those years, so my opportunities to influence his thinking were limited. I suppose it comes down to the nature versus nurture argument, but it is stunning to me how little we really do understand about how all of this works.

In the same vein dreams are a big deal in my mother's family, so from her, I learned dreams are not something to be dismissed because I ate too many tacos before I went to bed. Too many times to count, I would get a phone call from my mother asking me if I was okay because she had a dream about me that upset her. I found that she was right about 95 percent of the time, not about the exact details of my troubles but there was "a disturbance in the force."

I too would get dreams. They were vivid and so real I was surprised when I woke up to discover I was dreaming (like the dream I had that I had died, but that is another story for another time). Unlike the other 95 percent of my dreams, these dreams did not pass from my consciousness once I passed from sleep to wakefulness but stayed with me—often for years. This story begins with one such dream. Because of the family belief in the importance of dreams, coming first with my maternal grandmother, Mary, I knew better than to ignore dreams like that. Interestingly, my youngest daughter Amanda has many more of these dreams than I do. She wants no part of them, so I hear little about them from her, *yet* she does go to mediums. Go figure!

I hope this chapter adds some depth to my story. My life perceptions are shaped by my worldview, my experiences, and perhaps, the dispositions that come with my genetic biology. I do not know exactly how all this work, but I can take advantage of the system to gain insight and understanding into my life. "Wait," you say how can you take advantage of a system you do not understand? That is easy because we all do it every day. I get in my car and turn the key, and I can get from point A to point B anytime I want. I have no clue how my car works beyond preventive maintenance, like changing the oil, but I can still operate it. The same is true with electric lights. I flip a switch, and as long as the power is connected, I can illuminate whatever I want. I can change a light bulb, but do I understand how alternating current works? Not a chance. From this, I have learned that the whole system works better when you give love and receive love in return.

Chapter 6

YANKEE DOODLE DANDY

> Yankee Doodle went to town
> Riding on a pony;
> He stuck a feather in his hat,
> And called it macaroni
> Yankee Doodle keep it up;
> Yankee Doodle dandy,
> Mind the music and the step,
> And with the girls be handy

The song/melody for this chapter is an American favorite that dates back to the Revolutionary War, and it does not have a copyright. I will not explain why it represents this chapter at this point. If you have read this far, you might even be pretty sure you already know. If not, you can be pretty sure I will tell you eventually.

Recently, I was watching a television program, and there was a scene with recovering servicemen with missing limbs. As part of their recovery, they were involved in a program called MusiCorps. The website identifies the program as "conservatory-level music rehabilitation program that helps wounded warriors play music and recover their lives" (http://musicorps.net). I cried. I was so deeply touched by these brave men, but I realized that my tears were coming from a very deep part of my psyche.

I realized my tears were much more than an emotional response to a moving program, and I knew this because I am writing this memoir. Back in my autobiographical chapter, "San Antonio Rose," I wrote this about my polio rehab. "I did my rebab at Fort Sam with World War II vets who had to learn to walk again because Fort Sam was where the worst cases were sent. My memories from that time are vague but pleasant. I was loved and protected by my 'military guard.'" As I shed my tears, I remembered writing these words, and I knew there was a connection between these men on TV and my "military guard." My tears came from a place of deep sadness for the loss of these precious men some sixty plus years ago.

It is astonishing to me that this memoir is helping me to uncover my own past; I thought I knew everything about that. For someone like me, who loves metaphor and paradox, this is astonishing and exciting. There are the obvious things in my past like recounting events in my life, my parents, siblings, and children. But for me to reach back to people and places that I have no conscious memory of was unexpected. (Remember I wrote earlier that I can flip a light switch and illuminate without knowing a single thing about alternating current?) The realization made me think more about leaving Texas so many years ago. I had to acknowledge an anger at being taken away from not only my father, who went to Europe, but also the comfort and surroundings at Fort Sam. I was brought to New York and to a house full of people, though my family, who were complete strangers.

This thread of thought is appropriate to begin this chapter about the Paige family because everywhere I look, there is the military. Of course, I begin with both my parents, my brother Bob, and two uncles in the military, and I did mention that I wanted to be in the military as well. My Dad had to gently explain that polio made that dream impossible. In my genealogical searching, I discovered that my father's sister Anne was in the Women's Army Corps. I have the draft registration card for my Pappy, but I am not sure he served because the card listed a cataract in his right eye. It appears great x 2 Grandfather Timothy (born in 1818) may have served in the Union Army during the Civil War. I believe these men are descended from

Colonel Timothy Paige (1727–1791) and his son Captain Timothy Paige (1757–1836) both in the Continental Army of the American Revolution. Back in the "Helter Skelter" chapter, I made mention of this lineage and the silly conclusion, on my part, that the Paige line of my family was straightforward.

By the time I finished writing the "Girl" chapter, I had hit yet another dead end with my grandmother Emma's family line. I suspected there was a second marriage before she married my grandfather because I found a marriage record. How did she get to Philadelphia to meet my grandfather? How did my grandfather get to Philadelphia, from Ohio where his draft registration was from? When and how did Pappy leave Vermont where he was born? I had no idea nor could I find a marriage license for Pappy and Emma. So even though I feel Emma is not done with me yet, I had to let that family line alone for now and refocus on the "easy" task of tracing the Paige clan.

I have written that if humility is a partner in our life, we will not so easily overlook things or become overconfident. I was feeling smug as I wrote, in "Helter Skelter," about untangling the confusion around the identity of my Pappy. If he was indeed the son of George Paige, who was the son of Timothy and Rebecca Paige, I could trace back to Colonel Timothy Paige of the Continental Army of the American Revolution. I did not want the genealogical headway I had made in the past months to be lost, so I decided to investigate membership in the Daughters of the American Revolution (DAR). I have a good friend Jane, who teaches writing, who is eligible to join the DAR. Jane also read some of this writing and encouraged me to publish. I asked Jane about her knowledge about the DAR and decided, "Why not?"

I went to the national website of the DAR. Sure enough, the patriot Timothy Paige has many of his female offspring as members of the organization. So I wrote a letter of inquiry requesting information on membership. Several months later, I received a phone call from a representative of the local organization. I requested, and she sent the membership information and the documentation requirements. OMG!

To begin with, they want birth, marriage, and death certificates for the last three generations. Okay, let's begin with my father. He was born, signed for Social Security, and enlisted in the army as Frank Albert. When he was discharged from the army and when he died, he was Frank Allen. His mother's name is Emma on his birth record, and Nancy O'Hara on his death certificate because my mother did not know her mother-in-law's real name.

For Pappy, I cannot find a Vermont birth record with his name on it. His death certificate lists his DOB as November 4, 1878, in Vermont, but the state of Vermont does not have a birth record for him on this date. There is a male birth record in Vermont for a son born to George and Louisa Paige on November 5, 1884. This is good because George is the name of the second son of Timothy and Rebecca Paige, but it seems the name George Paige is the John Smith of Vermont. I must prove that my great-grandfather is George Paige and that he is the George Paige who is the son of Timothy and Rebecca. More on this later.

I have a draft registration for Frank Albert, DOB November 4, 1884 (okay, so it is only one day off), and he identifies his nearest relative as George Paige in Proctorsville, Vermont. I do have a marriage certificate for George Paige and Louise Blanchard and a Social Security application in 1935 where Frank Paige (DOB November 4, 1885—Okay, so it is one year off—again) and George and Louisa are listed as his parents.

In case you have not noticed, I do not have two pieces of paper with the same DOB for Pappy. In addition, I cannot find a marriage record for Pappy and Emma. I do believe I might have an idea why Pappy's death certificate shows 1878 as his DOB. If he is sixty-eight at the time of his hospitalization, he might be eligible for more social security and/or health benefits than he would receive if he was sixty-two. All I have is my ever-increasing imagination to support this theory, but I think it is as good as any. What will the DAR accept? Only God knows the answer to that, and now, He is silent.

Then there is George, my great-grandfather. George, the son of Timothy and Rebecca, was born in 1846–1847. For all the George Paige's there are in Vermont, there are no birth records, at least ones that I can find. I do have census records that show that Timothy and Rebecca's George was their firstborn son, and he was three years old on the 1850 census. In 1870, he was twenty-three years old and still living with his parents and siblings. The marriage record for George and Louise (July 3, 1875) shows the same residence information that I found on Pappy's unnamed birth certificate of November 5, 1884. The marriage record shows George's parents as J and R Paige. I think the J was a mistake, and it was supposed to be a T for Timothy, and of course the R is Rebecca. The 1880 census shows George and Louisa with a one-year-old son, George Jr. I cannot find an 1890 census record for the family, and by 1895 George, son of Timothy and Rebecca, is marrying again to Mary Haskins, and then in the 1900 census, George is listed as widowed and living with his sister Martha Paige Parker.

As if all of this is not enough, there is an inaccurate timeline for George and Louisa on the genealogy websites. It shows that George and Louisa married on the same date as my great grandparents (I hope they are at least), married for fifty years, having a son George Jr. born on 1886, and George Sr. is the son of Timothy Paige. I have documented evidence that George Jr. was born in 1879 because he is on the 1880 census records. I have a copy of a marriage record for George, the son of Timothy and Rebecca, to a woman named Mary in 1895; he was widowed in 1900. When I first saw the timeline, I was ready to throw in the towel. I had dinner with my friend Jane and covered the restaurant table with my mass of paper hoping her "fresh eyes" would see something I missed. She did not.

I spent a week wallowing and despondent because this timeline changed *everything*. Maybe I could trace back to a patriot, maybe even the colonel, but now I had to rethink everything. I finally talked myself into looking at what I had to pick up the chase yet again. I compared my information to the information I had on the timeline. In a flash of insight-kind of like, I was not seeing the trees because of the forest; I realized that the timeline had to be wrong in some respects. I had information in my hand that proved some of my points. The George of this timeline was not the son of Timothy and Rebecca; they could not have it both ways. The bottom line was it had never occurred to me to question the veracity of the data presented online. I had become a cliché, and this experience left me wondering if anyone really checks online data. It is worse because others draw off the posted timeline, and the error is compounded.

Oh, by the way, have you figured out "Yankee Doodle" yet? Of course, I am considering the DAR and swimming in paper trying to relate my progenitors to a patriot who fought for independence back in 1776 and served on the Committee of Correspondence. (If that sounds familiar, get out your digital gizmos and look it up.) As I take a moment to look back on all the information, I have uncovered in the past twenty-five years, I am amazed at what I have learned, *but* I really think I have more questions today than I had twenty-five years ago. I keep pulling the thread, and it keeps unraveling in the most unexpected ways like why does sticking a feather in one's cap make it macaroni?

Chapter 7

IT'S RAINING MEN

> I'm gonna go out I'm gonna let myself get
> Absolutely soaking wet It's raining men
> Hallelujah
> It's raining men—every specimen Tall, blonde,
>   dark and lean
> Rough and tough and strong and mean
> (Paul Jabara and Paul Shaffer (1979), *It's Raining
>   Men*)

Yet again, this story takes an unexpected turn, hence my decision to begin a new chapter. I have admitted to having three husbands. I believe this is a clear indication that I do like men even if I show a marked lack of good judgment in the selection process. In fact, I openly admit I prefer the company of men to the company of women. I love sports and a good sense of humor, and I find male banter wonderful and invigorating. Maybe this too is a lingering artifact from my rebab days with my "military guard" at Fort Sam. At any rate, the image of "raining men," for me, is a pleasant thought indeed.

When I hear this lyric, I want to get up and dance with or without a disco ball shimmering over my head. I had years of unhampered mobility from my polio, so dancing was on my list of favorite things to do. As a child, I wanted to take dance lessons like my friends, but my mom said I could not do dance moves with a fused ankle. However, that did not stop me from dancing with my friends, and husbands, at every opportunity. Dancing is now near the top of my list of things to do when I pass into the next existence; I call it the golden bucket list. In that iteration, I am dancing with all the men of this chapter if they (and hopefully me) made the cut to the happy place.

The desire to dance aside this chapter is about the men in my line who led back to the patriot Colonel Timothy Paige and his patriot son Captain Timothy Paige, both Continental Army, Massachusetts Militia. I think it interesting that the only daughter in this line is me. Of course, they had female children; Colonel Timothy Paige had three daughters. However, I come down the line with the name Paige intact from my patriot ancestor, so it is "raining men" of all kinds. As I type these words, it is raining outside, quite heavily I might add, which makes the metaphor complete. In addition, while I have not conducted an exhaustive analysis of the DAR records, it seems this direct lineage is rather unusual.

I chose to go back to the Paige name over twenty years ago long before this DAR application was even conceived in me. You can imagine how confusing the life of an academic is when one is dealing with three marriages. My undergraduate degree bears the surname of husband 1, master's degree bears the surname of husband 2, professional certifications bear the name of husband 3, and for my PhD, I came full circle back to my birth name: Susan Mary Paige. Confusion aside, the most difficult part of all of this, for me, is having to admit I had three husbands; at least I had them one at a time.

Once again, I remind you about the foolish statement I wrote in a prior chapter about how the Paige genealogy was straightforward. I saw all of those men, and it all seemed so clear-cut. The previous chapter outlined the ambiguity and frustration I experienced as I tried to organize the material I was following. I also wrote about my frustrating experience with an online timeline I found about my great-grandfather George Paige. At first, I thought this "straightforward" search was over, and my DAR aspirations were smashed. At that point though, I still had a family line to trace it was not the one I suspected I had. Truth be told, I saw Colonel Timothy Paige as a desirable ancestor, an officer, and a gentleman, and I was sad to lose him.

I guess I should insert here that my mother did not think much of my father's background; she was of Polish Catholic descent. She referred to Dad as a "shanty Irishman," and now, the joke is on her. I do not think there is much Irish—let alone Catholic—DNA in this group of Paige men. They are WASP (White Anglo-Saxon Protestant) to the bone. I am sure my father's marriage to a Polish Catholic set off some seismic disturbances back about seven or eight generations on the "other side." I did suggest that was one of the reasons my father married her—giving the figurative middle finger to those who saw him as an inferior link in the Paige line.

The Bible refers to a "cloud of witnesses" (Hebrews 12:1) who watch our lives here, and I am convinced they have been observing my odyssey with interest. Remember my grandmother Emma's request of me to bring the family together? In a way, I am even now doing just that. In addition, my mom's dismissive attitude toward the Paige family has so much irony attached to it I cannot adequately put it into words. She would tell me I was "just like my father," and it was never meant as a compliment. With Colonel Timothy Paige in the genealogy, it was really the nicest thing she could say to me. It makes a nice Catholic girl like me believe in *karma*. So you can see why I was deeply unhappy with the doubt the timeline created.

So to pick up my narrative, I persisted in this state of frustration for about a week and then I picked up my work and looked at the data I had collected. The US Census was clear: Great Grandpa George had a son, George Jr., born in 1878 because he was on the 1880 Census. The birth certificate I had for the nameless male child—born to George and Louisa, November 4, 1884—was quite possibly Pappy. I needed to have my great-grandfather George be the son of Timothy and Rebecca Richardson Osborn Paige because this was my direct bloodline to the Colonel Timothy Paige and the DAR. Yet the timeline I saw, though it clearly indicated that this George Paige was the son of Timothy and Rebecca, indicated a single son to George and Louisa.

Then I found an 1895 marriage record for George, son of Timothy and Rebecca, and on the 1900 US Census, he is a widow, but there was no sign of Pappy. Even if Timothy and Rebecca were not my great, great grandparents, it was clear that the George in the online timeline did not line up with the facts. The whole thing was complicated by the fact that I could not find a birth or a death record for Great-Grandmother Louisa. The DAR wants birth, death, and marriage records for the first three generations back from me so this was going to be a problem. Did Great-Grandmother Louisa die in childbirth? That might explain why there was no name on the 1884 birth certificate for a male child. In any case, Louisa was dead, or possibly divorced by 1895, so was Pappy sent to live with a foster family? It is interesting to note that when Grandma Emma died, my seven-year-old father was put in foster care by Pappy.

This reexamined information gave me renewed energy to find the link between this George and Louisa and my Pappy. I was over my disappointment in the faulty timeline, but when I did a search, this timeline kept coming up, so now, I was annoyed. First, this timeline was the source of my emotional discomfort for an entire week; I am too busy for such things. Second, every time it came up as part of my search results, it made me question the veracity of the other data I was encountering. Remember the part I wrote about humility as a necessary companion on such a quest as this? Well, I gave *her* the day off on the day I wrote an email to the author of the online timeline. My purpose was to explain the errors of their ways and somewhat respectfully request that they change it because it was "messing up my searches."

I watched my inbox for a response for several days, but I did not receive a response from the timeline folks. Two things happened in the interim. The first was I found a record for a 1935 Social Security application for Pappy where he listed a DOB of November 4, 1885; of course, you could not expect it to match the date on any of the other documents I had for Pappy. What it did list was the names of George and Louisa as his parents. This was the link I needed to circle back to proving the nameless birth certificate was indeed Pappy's, and hence Timothy and Rebecca were his grandparents.

The second thing that happened was I contacted my DAR representative requesting a meeting. I had collected a massive amount of paper documentation, but some of it did not exactly match documents the DAR was requiring like the records for the three generations back from me. You will be happy to know Humility was back from *her* hiatus, and so I determined that I needed to be sure that (a) I was still eligible for membership, (b) I was on the right track, (c) I knew what else I had to do and/or collect, and (d) what the heck did the DAR do anyway? Basically, her answers were (a) Yes, (b) Yes, (c) Not much, and (d) meeting schedules and places.

On a Friday, I sent a second email to the timeline folks and tried to be more diplomatic in telling them how wrong they were, and by Sunday, I had a response. The timeline folks, now known as Marcia, expressed confusion over what I was conveying to them. I took over two hours, remember the two-finger typing, to write a reasoned and logical description of my position and the data I had to support it. The next day, I had my DAR meeting, and on Tuesday, when I returned from work, the light on my answering machine was flashing.

I have a standard signature line on my email that contains my home phone number, and I often forget it is there. The flashing light on my answering machine was indicating that I had a message from Marcia asking me to call her to answer some questions. There was a small part of me that was annoyed because I thought I had been crystal clear. How could she possibly be confused? You are reading this memoir, so my clarity of thought must be apparent to you.

Another part of me was wondering if I had opened a whole can of worms. Was I going to be accused of besmirching the memory of her grandfather by suggesting that his life was not quite as the timeline suggested? After all, I was suggesting another wife and a son no one seemed to know about. Before I responded to the call, I did grab my folder so my data was right in front of me if I was challenged. Sometimes, our minds take us to some silly places, and I am happy to report these fears were quickly allayed.

Marcia told me she looked up the documents I had written about (the marriage register, the birth certificate of the unnamed male child, etc.), and she found they existed as described. (I told you I was crystal clear!) However, in retrospect, I realized that telling someone that the family narrative, which they had believed for many years, had errors does not mean that the person accepts the new reality in an instant. If you need a reminder of this, go back to the beginning of this chapter. This whole memoir is about me discovering this very truth, yet I expected that by simply telling Marcia her revised family history was a *fait accompli*—another lesson learned in this very crazy venture.

I will not recount the whole dialogue between Marcia and I, but suffice it to say that her grandfather and Pappy were brothers. That realization was an epic shift in both our worlds. For me, this was the second time in three months I found family I never knew I had. Marcia needed to change her timeline, but now, she too wanted to join DAR as well. She did mention she thought that there might have been some family talk that her grandfather had a brother and she did contact her uncle to find out if her grandfather George had a younger brother.

Marcia emailed to tell me that her uncle indeed had confirmed his father had a brother; his name was Frank, and everyone lost track of him. She wrote:

> I spoke with my Uncle Tim (OMG! His name is Timothy Paige!) this morning, and he confirmed that yes, his father did have a brother named Frank, but that he never met him. He said all that he knew was that Frank was "well-to-do" and was in the "textile industry." He didn't know how Frank came to be in Ohio. Sorry that I couldn't learn more, but that was all that he knew. (Personal Communication)

Now you are thinking, *This is wonderful!* Well, not really. Yes, it is wonderful to find this whole new branch of the family. It confirms the documentation I have collected, so Timothy and Rebecca are my great, great grandparents—DAR, here I come, right? It certainly expands Emma's message to me in ways I *never* anticipated, and I really feel small in the face of all of this.

However, if you remember back in "Helter Skelter," I had managed to separate the two Franks: Frank Albert (aka Pappy) and Frank Hill Paige. Timothy and Rebecca had two sons, George, my great-grandfather, and Edwin. Both men had sons they named Frank. My Pappy is the second son of George Paige—Frank Albert (November 4, 1884). Edwin's son is Frank Hill Paige (September 29, 1878). So far, you are thinking that I am making difficulty where none exists. I just call your attention to the description of the missing Frank in the email. The Frank described there is Frank Hill Paige!

Frank Hill Page was involved in the wool business as were many of the Paige men, except Pappy. I have a copy of Frank Hill Paige's passport application and documentation of his travels with his mother Ella to buy wool in South America and Europe. My dad always talked about Pappy being in the restaurant and bar trade. His occupation on his death certificate is listed as a cook and on his draft registration as a waiter. I was struck the minute I read the email that the Frank Marcia's uncle described was Frank Hill Paige. Remember Pappy's death certificate listed his DOB as 1878—the year Frank Hill Paige was born.

I thought I had untangled that thread, and now it was all mixed up again. My DAR application was clear either way, but who the hell was Pappy? In addition, I return to the comment my former neighbor made when I showed her the pictures of a man who I believed to be Pappy. She said that she did not know who the people in the picture were, but they had money; she could tell by the clothes. I am familiar with these two Frank Paige's because I studied them for years. Until I read this email, I had felt certain that I had parsed out their identities. Now, not so much.

I am learning through all of this that a war is won with small battles—a little military lingo is appropriate here, I think—and overall, I had won some significant encounters. I was indeed the great-great-great-great-great granddaughter of Colonel Timothy Paige, so I have submitted my paperwork to the local DAR affiliate for audit and approval prior to sending the application to Washington, DC, for final approval. I did finally find a death certificate for my paternal great-grandmother Louisa on the same day I was to turn over the paperwork—one last search and I hit gold. She died in 1886 of consumption when Pappy was a little more than one year old. I think Pappy was put into a type of foster care with family because he was so young when Louisa died.

    Finally, I made an extra copy of her death certificate to send to Marcia to help her correct the timeline for Louisa.

Chapter 8

ANNIE'S SONG

> You fill up my senses
> Like a night in a forest
> Like the mountains in springtime
> Like a walk in the rain
> Like a storm in the desert
> Like a sleepy blue ocean
> You fill up my senses
> Come fill me again
> (John Denver [1974] *Back Home Again*)

This song lyric is a no-brainer because this chapter is about my father's sister and my Aunt Anne Louise Paige, and of course the lyric is part of "Annie's Song." Let us go back to 1977 to set the scene and notice "Annie's Song" had already been recorded by that date. My father had died about two months ago, and I had just saved the famous cigar box from the trash heap. I was sitting in the screened patio room in the rear of my parents' house on a summer day looking at the contents of the cigar box. I was fascinated by the unmarked pictures, but the first thing I could identify was a birth certificate.

It was an original birth certificate, with an embossed seal, for Anne Louise Paige (of course, the significance of her middle name, Louise, took almost forty years to be grasped by me). Her parents were Frank Albert Paige (Albert?) and (What? Who? Wait?), and her DOB was October 2, 1924 (Younger? Not Nancy?).

Now you need to understand that it was just two months before my mother listed the name of Dad's mother, her own mother-in-law, as Nancy O'Hara on his death certificate. Just recently, I obtained a copy of his death certificate for the DAR documentation, and I was really surprised to see this. I often wondered if Mom knew more about Dad's family than she was letting on, but seeing this entry on his death certificate makes me think less and less that this is true. My mother could be devious, but this kind of forethought to promote disinformation was beyond even her remarkable skills. Besides, she gave me the cigar box that contained the birth certificate, and that too is significant. I think if she really realized the implications of that birth certificate, I would never have seen it. I think apathy on her part about the whole subject is a more likely explanation.

At the time, the worst part of seeing this birth certificate was the realization that my dad had to know, and he was lying to us. This birth certificate was in *his* cigar box. The intensity of the moment is indicated by the clarity of my memory some forty years later. I knew if I said too much, my mother might find a way to take the box away, so I put it down on the picnic table bench next to me. Besides, I had to process what I had found. I had no idea how long that was going to take or that one day I would be writing a book chapter about my Aunt Anne and all the things I still do not know.

You need to understand that in the greater story of my life, Aunt Anne's existence was a minor discovery at the time: (a) I had not had *the dream*. (b) I had another marriage and two divorces to go through. (c) I was going to move across New York State to the Mohawk Valley for twelve years where I would have the dream. (Also thirty years later, I would learn that the progenitors of the Paige clan, Nathaniel and Christopher Paige, were part of the history of that area.) When I returned to WNY, I was a Paige again, divorced, unemployed, and had a pregnant sixteen-year-old daughter who refused to leave the Mohawk Valley. Amid all of this ruin, I went back to university to earn a PhD and became Dr. Susan Mary Paige in May of 2003.

During those years, I would return to the cigar box. Most of the time, I would spend about thirty minutes trying to will some insight into the pictures so I would know who these people were. I knew over half of them were WWII photos of friends and places my dad encountered, so the number of mysteries diminished, but the percentage of knowledge about the rest remained zero. That did not seem like progress to me.

As I chronicled in the first chapter, I first focused on finding Pappy in the early 1990s. I still marvel at the miracle of me using my father's stories about Pappy's involvement in the Elks Club, the Elks Club booklet in the cigar box, and a scrap of information I found online about cemeteries having an Elk Rest section to locate Mount Mariah Cemetery. Then to write to the people in charge of the cemetery and actually get a response that located his burial plot goes right to the top of the list of "Believe it or Not." Then I was able to send to Vital Records in Philadelphia to get Pappy's death certificate. When I realized how old he was when he died, I did get an insight, and I knew who he was in the pictures. What a breakthrough!

Flushed with the pride of victory, I thought since I had so much success with locating Pappy's death certificate, I should order a birth record for Anne. After all, I had an original, but it was in rough shape, so another official record sounded like a good idea. So I filled out the form, wrote the check, and sent my request to Vital Records. After the usual month wait, I received a letter that this record did not exist. What? I had an original in my possession; how could this be? It made no sense to me. Is this the agony of defeat? Of course, I was going through all the other life experiences chronicled above, so this mystery was put on the back burner yet again.

Several years later, I was relating this story to my friend Gill who does a fair amount of genealogical work herself, and she said she would look for me. She came back puzzled and said she could find no trace of Anne Louise Paige. Rob, who met me at Mount Mariah to visit my Pappy's grave, took up the challenge and could find nothing. I used to quip about a witness protection program, and both Gill and Rob thought that possibility was looking more and more likely because nothing else came close to explaining the complete lack of information.

One lovely spring day in 2013, I was between classes, sitting outdoors, and thinking about my Aunt Anne. I went back to my computer with a "What the heck!" attitude, did a *Google* search for her, and, unlike the other one hundred times I had done this, I got a hit for an Anne L. Paige—a military record. "Why not?" I thought. The colonel and the captain were not on my radar yet, but both my parents were in the military, so why not Anne? The DOB was October 2, 1923, not 1924, but the answer soon came. Aunt Anne lied about her age to get into the Women's Army Corps (WAC); she made herself old enough for enlistment. Besides, Dad said the Red Cross could not find his sister for Pappy's funeral; the Red Cross looks for military personnel. "Gotcha, Dad!"

My search skills went into high gear, and I found the form to request military records and wrote a cover letter explaining that Anne L. Paige was my aunt, and I was requesting her records for genealogical reasons. I waited patiently, but I was disappointed at the end. It seemed the fire that had all but destroyed my dad's military records had destroyed her records. The only available record containing her name was a final payment roll. This was a sign-off list of military personnel who were being discharged on September 10, 1948, from Fort Meade, Maryland.

When Anne entered the army in November 1944, she had completed two years of high school, and her civilian occupation was listed as semiskilled machine shop. This makes me smile because during marriage 1 and 2 and while completing undergraduate and master's degrees, I worked in a small manufacturing operation where I eventually became the bookkeeper. I loved this job. Anne was a corporal and got an early release. It appeared the army provided her with funds to return to Philadelphia, yet her forwarding address was to a location that is a funeral service today. I did contact the funeral service and learned that in 1948, the location had been a private residence, a big private residence, I might add. Pappy had died in March of 1947, so where was she going? Did she think of Dad? Did she try to contact him? Did I mention that Dad's military records listed her as next of kin and beneficiary if Pappy died while he was in the military? I checked the address Dad had listed for her in 1942 at Wyncote, Pennsylvania, and it was a 2,500 square feet Colonial, built in 1931, and worth about $350,000 in today's market. Whose house was this because it was not the same address he listed for Pappy in Philadelphia? The house was five miles from the center of Philadelphia. They *had* to have some contact. Gosh, my head was spinning.

After this spirt of information all hits on her name went back into the ether. Then in the summer of 2015, one of the genealogy sites had a free access weekend. As I always did, I began my search with Grandma Emma, and that is when her death certificate and her stunning cause of death was revealed to me. As an afterthought, I also did a search for Aunt Anne, and a Social Security Death Index came up. I have not mentioned this, but all through this process, I was hoping Aunt Anne was still alive, but now, I knew she died in May of 1988, and her married name was Bailey. I made a joke to Gill that I hoped her husband's name was George (get it? George Bailey?), but it was not to be; it was Owen. I was sad to know of her death.

I learned that my uncle's name was Owen on Aunt Anne's death certificate. I do not want to sound ghoulish, but I love death certificates because they are a treasure trove of information. She lived and died in Philadelphia. Pappy's name was there, but under mother's maiden name was unknown. I felt so bad for Grandma Emma because she was left out of her mother's obituary and now her daughter's death certificate. Aunt Anne was a little over four years old when Emma died but the name listed on her Social Security application next to mother's name is a match so she did acknowledge Grandma Emma at some point.

I was curious about the informant for the information on the death certificate. This person and Aunt Anne had the same address, so perhaps, it was one of her children—my first cousin. She was cremated, so I do not know if there is a grave site to visit. Her occupation was accountant at the time of her death, imagine that. Remember I told you about my job in a small manufacturing plant that turned into my becoming a bookkeeper? Not exactly the same, but I love keeping books, and so did Dad. I do all my own taxes and would have been happy in my bookkeeping job. Of course, now, it is all excel, not those lovely ledger books. Oh, by the way, Dad was a skillful bookkeeper as well; he was quartermaster at the veterans' club he managed.

There is no way that I can be positive, but I feel strongly that Aunt Anne was met by Pappy and Grandma Emma when she passed over. Hopefully, Dad was there too. It had been a long time since they had been together, and they all had catching up and explaining to do. I have referenced before that during the passage to the next existence, I believe the "blinders" we have in this life are gone. We all see how petty our hurts, anger, jealously, and bitterness really were. Because we are no longer carrying all the excess baggage we had in this life, our real selves are what everyone sees in us when we meet again. There is only room for joy in this most intimate of reunions.

The lyric of "Annie's Song" presents metaphors about how one feels when they love a girl named Annie. I believe, in a similar fashion, that the next life will fill all our senses in much the same way. I also believe that our disappointments will be explained or just simply be forgotten. Now, some of you might challenge my view of the next life or Heaven or the cloud as I like to call it. If it was more of the same life in this existence, I am not too sure I would continue to strive for it.

In one of my favorite movies, *City of Angels,* the angel Seth (played by Nicholas Cage) asks the doctor Maggie (Meg Ryan) if she believes we are just cells and tissue. When she replies that she sees no other options, Seth asks her, "How do you explain the enduring myth in Heaven?" That is the perfect thought to end this chapter.

Chapter 9

AMAZING GRACE

When we've been there ten thousand years,
Bright shining as the sun,
We've no less days to sing God's praise
Than when we first begun
(John Newton [1779])

Of course, this song lyric is the last verse of "Amazing Grace." Time is an interesting phenomenon that we all experience and yet we really do not grasp except in terms of our limited sphere of existence. Men and women have long conjectured on time travel and its consequence, and I find myself particularly drawn to movies about this topic: *Time After Time* (1979), *Somewhere in Time* (1980), *Back to the Future* (1985, 1989, 1990), *The Lake House* (2006), *Déjà Vu* (2006), *Interstellar* (2014). Now, the idea of time travel to solve my unanswered genealogy questions, though incredibly appealing, is not an option currently open to me. However, my belief system includes ideas that can transcend time and distance, and this chapter explores this idea.

Remember I said Dad was always comfortable with the wealthy while my mom wanted to run and hide from them? Dad golfed with lawyers, judges, and businessmen and felt right at home with them at a country club. I believe this is more amazing because Dad had a speech impediment, a stutter, yet his strength was his sense of humor.

Dad's first date with my mother was to take her to the opera of all places. I believe for all his repudiation of his family, in particular Pappy, Dad was more a Paige than he wanted to admit. If I may use a well-worn cliché, blood is thicker than water. In a prior chapter, I have pointed out the similarities between Dad and the half-sister he never knew: Edna Ruth.

In addition, Dad had an amazing amount of cultural capital.

> The term cultural capital refers to non-financial social assets that promote social mobility beyond economic means. Examples can include education, intellect, and style of speech, dress, or physical appearance. (Wikipedia)

These assets also include table manners and etiquette. These attributes set up a cultural milieu that working-class people simply do not understand, hence my mother's desire to hide. She felt out of place while Dad *never* did.

I came to this knowledge through my friend Gill. She was born in England where class distinctions are more overt. In the beginning, I was skeptical of the idea, but as we proceeded through our doctoral program, this template became more and more apparent. Eventually, we conducted some peer-reviewed published research on working-class women in PhD programs. It took me years of reflection and sorting to realize how different my parents were in this regard and then identify what was passed on to me. My standard quip is, "Last year, I did not know what cultural capital was, and now, I am scared to death of a *faux pas* in a social setting." This is particularly true in academia because many a promotion has been lost because of these social errors. (See the movie *The Rewrite* 2014.)

I think my PhD, both the process and the final product, was in keeping with the Paige family tradition of service and professionalism. I demonstrated the family mark of intelligence and leadership. That being said, I do not dismiss the great benefits that came from my polio and my working-class family—a solid work ethic. The mantra of polio rehabilitation in the 1950s was "No pain, no gain."

My mother and her working-class brothers worked hard and did whatever it took to accomplish their goals, and *no* whining allowed. The only ailment that stopped them might be the loss of a body part, but even that depended on if you could still work without it.

I believe my attitudes and my prayers got the attention of my relatives on the "other side." Now you are asking, "What does she mean by that?" Remember what I wrote about time a few paragraphs back? In the introduction, I addressed my worldview and the *communion of saints*. As I discovered each one of the ancestors, I began to pray for the repose of their souls. I named the unborn child Grandma Emma and Pappy had. He is Uncle George (I bet you thought I might name him Timothy) and included him in my daily prayers. In the case of Emma, Pappy, and Aunt Anne, I have Masses said for them every year on the anniversary of their death's just like I do for my parents and my mother's family. In my daily prayers, I remembered the Paige line back to the very Protestant Nathaniel and Christopher Paige. I must admit that when I include them in my prayers, I remind them that even though my Polish Catholic mother might be a scandal in the Paige line, her Catholic daughter says more prayers for them than they would ever get from their Protestant kin.

I know this might sound contrived to make this a better story, but I have a sense that my struggles and prayers got the attention of more than Grandma Emma; more on that later. I told you I believed that my parents' marriage was a large middle finger extended to Pappy and those who came before him by my dad. Dad was bitter because of his placement in a foster home, although Dad claimed Pappy kept his sister. Dad also claimed that the aftereffects of his spinal meningitis made him less of a "man" in Pappy's eyes. To prove himself, Dad joined the army and served as a medical corpsman in World War II in some of the worst fighting in the war, including North Africa and Anzio, Italy. Sadly, I heard him tell this story at an AA meeting I attended with him; he did not tell me directly. After the war, he returned to Philadelphia to work with his father. Pappy's attitude toward him did not appear to change, so he reenlisted, was stationed in San Antonio at Brooke Army Hospital, met my mother, and the rest, as they say, is history.

The colonel (Timothy Paige) was a lawyer as was his son, the captain (Timothy Paige). When they were not lawyering, the male Paiges were working in the wool/textile industry. Frank Hill Paige was a world traveler for the wool business. My father was the opposite end of this spectrum, as a high school dropout and with a military GED, *but* my dad believed in education, and he had high degree of cultural capital. I dedicated my doctoral dissertation to him because he loved all things school and encouraged me throughout his life. It was his encouragement and financial support that gave me the idea that I could advance my education as far as I wanted. My mother, on the other hand, wanted to have me committed to Sunny View.

My point here is that as I slowly worked my way through this journey of discovery, I began to work the new names and personalities into my life and prayers. For example, one evening, I was thinking about Pappy and wondering if Dad got to Philadelphia before he died. Dad never mentioned it, so I thought even if he had been there, I am not sure if they had much to say to one another. I imagined myself at Pappy's hospital bedside and began offering prayers for his consolation and spiritual comfort as he passed from this world so he did not feel so alone.

Another incident occurred when I finally traveled to Philadelphia to visit Pappy's grave. While I was there, I saw or rather felt the scene the day Pappy was buried, on a cold and blustery March day, and the loss and confusion felt by my father as he stood next to the open grave; I said prayers for Dad as well.

I am no prophet and/or seer, but I suspect some of you are rolling your eyes and thinking, *Oh, Brother*! I will try to explain this simply, but even that is a daunting task. I believe God is timeless, and He inhabits yesterday, today, and tomorrow simultaneously. I am not alone in this belief, but I do not want to turn this into a theological treatise. Years before I felt God had shown me that my prayers *today* could be applied to my dad at the moment of his death years before, that thought helped me to see I should not miss an important moment in time. God exists in a timeless realm, and He knows all and can apply all whenever He wants.

Besides, once they were together on the *other side*, the misunderstanding and hurt feelings were understood and forgiven. Pappy was reunited to his mother Louisa who died when he was barely one year old. Dad was reunited to his mother Emma who died when he was not quite seven years old. Pappy and Emma were reunited, and hopefully, Lysel and John made peace with them both. Everyone was coming together and watching their offspring, with the help of their guardian angles, became their focus. Because of my belief system, I know I am not alone in this single-minded ancestry quest.

There is another wonderful Catholic teaching that the personal guardian angels that we all have are our companions for eternity. They keep those who have passed informed about who is praying for them and what is going on with them back here on earth. So based on my belief system, I have an active communication system, *sans* medium. The Catholic Church holds prayers for the dead in high esteem and considers them a spiritual work of mercy. I had spent several decades actively including prayers and Masses for the dead as part of my personal spiritual practices. So as I learned of the new family members, I folded them into this practice. There is a family antidote that supports this belief.

In the years after Dad had died, Mom would have a Mass said for him on the anniversary of his death. I would come to her house, and we would attend the Mass together. About five years after he died, I asked about when the Mass was scheduled for that year. She told me that she did not think Dad needed it anymore and had not scheduled the Mass. Within a week, she had a dream about Dad. He was lying on the floor, and as she tried to step around him, he grabbed her ankle. She could not get away from him and awoke from the dream screaming and all wrapped in bedsheets. She went to the church the next day and scheduled the Mass. The bottom line of her decision was about the money for the Mass stipend, and she knew she had made a mistake.

Did I mention that dreams are a big deal in my family? That, along with my Catholic faith, come from my mother and maternal grandmother, Mary. Now, I am not talking about your garden variety dream of being naked in front of a classroom full of your friends.

These are full color, high-definition, high pixel-count dreams that even come with a soundtrack sometimes. These are dreams that are as real in twenty years as they were the night they happened—like say the dream I had of Grandma Emma. Often, I would get a call from my mother asking, "Are you alright?" Her call was prompted by a bad dream about me the night before, and she needed to call to see if I was *okay*. She was about 95 percent right in asking if I had a problem. She was right the other 5 percent too, but I lied to keep her from worrying about me, or I did not want to admit I had screwed up yet again.

It is this thinking that led me to believe I had a connection with, dare I say, the Paige *cloud*. Now I ask you why not call it the *cloud?* Nowadays, everything is in the *cloud*, so why not my ancestors? Besides some of the images of Heaven, clouds are a big part of the motif. I recently heard a discussion about the other place (a.k.a. Hell). Many of the philosopher/theologians suggest that in Hell, all personal identity is lost along with any connection to this realm. I should add here that this is another area where my worldview differs from the spiritualist. Though we both believe in an existence beyond this mortal plane, I believe that everyone is weighed and sent to the placement that they prepared for in this life. It is only fair, right?

As I ponder all of this, I am astonished, not that my grandmother Emma asked me to bring us all together, at the complexity and layers of meaning involved in that seemingly simple request. I had no idea where I would go, but I will say, though some of it was frustrating, I do not regret a single moment of the journey.

Chapter 10

SPEAK SOFTLY, LOVE

>Speak softly, love
>And hold me warm against your heart
>I feel your words
>The tender trembling moments start
>We're in a world, our very own
>Sharing a love that only few have ever known
>(Larry Kusik [1972])

This lyric might not strike a chord (I am so funny) with you; however, if you heard the melody, you would recognize it immediately. As I go along in this chapter, it will become apparent why I selected this lyric and melody. At this point, all I will say is I do not believe the Irish have a version.

So it seems I have hit a lull in my family quest. My DAR paperwork was submitted, and there was a letdown after that. The genealogical search was exhilarating, and for a time, it was fast-paced and a thrill a minute. You could tell by my narrative, right? Now I have to wait for the local and the national DAR to make a decision about my family line to the colonel. For a while, there I was, buried in paper and somewhat stressed by the gathering of the required documentation, and now—wait for it—I am bored.

In the past six months, I have discovered two branches to the family. I find it interesting that both of the branches have gone quiet.

Of course, in the case of my great granddad George's offspring, I am not so sure the discovery of me/us was the great news to them as it was to me. Now, why would I think this way? That is easy; I have a touch of paranoia. This is nothing that has been formally diagnosed. Besides, I was also told you are only paranoid if you are wrong.

I do not always make irrational claims, so let me set forth the evidence. I have chronicled my angst over their timelines (pardon me), inaccurate timelines:

1. In my third email to Marcia, I set out the historical documents I had gathered on my Pappy, and during our phone call, Marcia indeed did find the same things. She *seemed* to agree our grandfathers were brothers.
2. I was concerned about the birthdate on the timeline for her Grandfather George showing a birth year of 1885 on the timeline (more on this later). She told me she knew his birth year was 1878.
3. I found Louisa's death certificate showing she died in 1886 of consumption, *and* I sent Marcia a copy.
4. I received a copy of my Pappy's original Social Security application showing George and Louisa as his parents. I sent a copy of this document to Marcia as well.

I just now checked the timelines for George and Louisa, and nothing seemed to have changed in the past month. Now, I am sure that busy people have other things to do with their time. The problem is that this type of behavior is simply feeding the beast that is my paranoia. I think about how I would react in her position. I have not created a public timeline, but I am writing a book with the hope it might someday be published. I ask myself, "Why is she so reluctant to make the changes?" Somehow, I cannot shake the feeling that a public connection to my Pappy may not be desirable. Her own uncle said his father had a brother. I reproduced the copy of his email for you rather than paraphrase his comments. Uncle Tim made Pappy sound like a wealthy *bon vivant*, so what is the shame to having him in the family?

In order to answer my own question, it is time to reveal some more family secrets. It is interesting to me how these things suddenly come to mind and fall into place where I need them. Let me begin by recounting that my dad always reminded everyone that, "You know it is not just Italians in the Mafia. There is an Irish and Jewish Mafia as well." Okay, that statement alone is like "So what?" Then in a different context, Dad would say, "My father ran a club in Philly during the Depression, and when everyone else was broke, he always had money." I bet my dad was dead almost twenty years when I realized that the Depression existed during Prohibition, so my Pappy's place was most likely a speakeasy! (denoting a place where unlicensed liquor sales were made [Wikipedia]). Who provided the liquor to the Speak Easys? It took me longer still to put these two statements together, but when I did, "Oh my!"

I have further proof beyond these musings. I had been pondering the implications of this connection for several years when I was watching a movie on TV about the Mafia with my mother. In all innocence, I said, "You know Dad always said there were more than Italians in the Mafia. I wonder if his father had ties to the Mafia." If I had hit my mother with a cattle prod, I do not think I would have gotten a more startled and angry response. She began, not by denying the truth in my utterance but rather, by saying, "Don't you ever repeat that to anyone. Don't tell your kids because they will tell people. Never mention this again." I can be slow on the uptake, and in this case, I was so stunned by the vehemence of her response I just dropped the subject for the moment. When I told my youngest brother and my cousin the story, she did not tell me not to tell them, they both had the same immediate response: "She knows something!"

What my mother did know, she took it to the grave with her in 2008 because I never brought up the topic again. If she ever had a thought that I might write this all in a book, she might have assisted my transition to the other side before the thought of writing occurred to me. (Perhaps, this suggests that the Polish had their own version of the Mafia, and then I find out her family are Russian Poles, and we know about the Russian mob!) Remember Marcia's Uncle Tim said his Uncle Frank was well-to-do. My former neighbor and my dad both said Pappy had money. I will also admit Dad kind of knew about stuff. "What stuff?" you ask. To protect the memory of the dead, I will just write that it may have included skills required to run a speakeasy.

If this is not enough to fuel my paranoia, I can add some more gasoline to the fire. Emma's father, Pappy's father-in-law, was in the higher echelon of the railroad unions in Pennsylvania. Dare I say that it is suggested that the Mafia was involved with the labor movement in this country? Anybody find Jimmy Hoffa yet? I have always wondered how Emma in Harrisburg met Pappy in Philadelphia. Maybe, this is the connection, and maybe, it is not, but if I have learned anything in this vision quest, it is that no clue should be ignored.

There is more however. When I received the copy of Pappy's Social Security application, he listed the name of his employer in 1935. So as not to leave any stone unturned, I put the employer's name in a genealogical site search engine. I came up with the employer's death certificate. His cause of death was, wait for it, homicide from a traumatic head injury caused by a hand (?). The ? was on the death certificate, and my first thought was, *Or a baseball bat.* The homicide occurred in a café up the street from the victim's apartment. You will be interested to know the address is a nail salon in Philadelphia today. Where would I be without Google maps? I searched the Philadelphia papers hoping to find more, but I was unable to locate anything.

I do not believe in coincidence. Individually, these events are meaningless; however, I would suggest to you that if you brought them all together, this is a major cluster of "you fill in the blank." There was one other unrelated piece, so I thought, I discovered, and then I thought it might not be so unrelated after all. My father's military records listed Aunt Anne's home address in 1942. I looked up the address in Wyncote, a northern suburb of Philadelphia, and I saw pictures of the house. It was for sale for about $375,000. No cold water walk-up or small shack in the woods for Anne. Was it Pappy's house? I do not think so because Pappy had a different address on the same papers. If not, whoever she was staying with had money. The house was built in 1931, and I could not find out who owned it in 1942; I wish I was a hacker. I do know some folks in law enforcement, so maybe I can get some tips on places to look.

I was able to ask someone in law enforcement about public sources of police records for someone who died in 1947. He told me files for anyone born before the 1950s were stored away, and a person needed authorization and a good reason to go looking for something. I sort of thought this was the way it worked. What he said next gave me the "ah-ha!" moment. The records were stored by the individual's birthdate. Remember my lament that no two pieces of paper about my Pappy had the same DOB? If someone, who lived prior to the digital age, wanted to keep his criminal activity scattered about so no one could compile all of his misdeeds in one place, what could he do? Even if my friend could look for me, what DOB do I use? Maybe I am giving my Pappy too much credit, but those who have any history and success in nefarious activities know how to work the system for their benefit. I think I know everything I need to know.

I am not done with this because in my downtime, I discovered one more *new* family bit of information. I began this chapter writing about how bored I was. I was sick of the searches because I was getting the same stuff repeatedly. I can find no marriage record for Pappy and Emma, and that is bothering me. My slot machine metaphor still hold true for genealogy search engines however. I did yet another search for Pappy and Emma hoping for a marriage record, and I did not find it? No. What I did find was stunning however. Pappy and Emma had a fourth child, counting Uncle George, and he was stillborn on July 31, 1926. They named him John, after Great-Granddad John, Emma's father.

How sad I was for Emma all over again. She gave up Edna/Ruth for adoption. Her marriage to Charles ended in divorce, and he was declared insane. Dad had spinal meningitis at age four, and now her second son is stillborn. As a mother, I cannot imagine how she felt. To carry a child to term and have him stillborn had to be devastating for her. She still had two small children to care for. Was Pappy understanding? What shape was their marriage in? If his career activities were of the illegal kind, then that did not make for wedded bliss. I would suggest that the end of Emma's next pregnancy was a good indicator of love on the rocks—cue, Neil Diamond for yet another lyric. All I could think about was that these events were like a constant water drip on a hard rock surface. In time, the incessant dripping creates, first, a small indentation and, as time passes, a gash that gets bigger and bigger. Drip, drip, drip…

So my song lyric for this chapter has a double meaning. The lyric is the theme from *The Godfather*, and it is clearly an illusion to the suspected link between Pappy and some *made* guys. But this piece of music is also a love theme. It represents not only the love between man and woman but also it can represent the love between mother and child. Pappy and Emma were clearly sharing the same bed, but was it love or something else? I would like to think there was some love between them, but that part of the story remained unknown to me. If I could just find the marriage record—dare I say—maybe, this would give me some more answers.

Chapter 11

SON OF A PREACHER MAN

> The only one who could ever reach me
> Was the son of a preacher man
> The only boy who could ever teach me
> Was the son of a preacher man
> Yes he was, he was, ooh, yes he was
> (John Hurley and Ronnie Wilkins [1968] *Dusty
>   in Memphis*)

Maybe I should calm down a bit before I write this. I wrote the last chapter yesterday; remember I was bored? Suffice it to say I was not bored today. I began the day doing a search like I always do just because I have done it so much in the past months it has simply become a habit. I had come across some information on Rev. Dr. Lucius Robinson Paige. He is the son of Captain Tim and the brother of Great-great-great-Granddad Martin Paige. He wrote a book that I ordered yesterday on the history of Massachusetts. I thought it would be helpful in my getting some more detail on the colonel and the boys. I printed a page from an online family history with details about him and glanced at it before I left work yesterday.

Two terms jumped out at me: *Universalist* and *33 Degree Free Mason* as I was walking out the door. Oh brother, that is just what a practicing Trinitarian Christian Roman Catholic wants to see in his or her ancestry. I was thinking I had some Methodists or Presbyterians back there with Nathaniel and Christopher Paige. That covers the Trinitarian and Christian part and something we could live with. I am orthodox in case you have not figured it out, and this is really important to me.

When I had time this morning, I went to my quick backup resource: Wikipedia. I found that back in 1823, when Rev. Dr. Paige was ordained, there was *some* Christian theology involved in the Universalist Church, and this was before the joining with the Unitarians. I will probably need to do some *real* research. *Wikipedia* is good place to begin my research, but they had a disclaimer on the section I was reading that the entry was incomplete, and they needed more input for accuracy. I do not think it takes a PhD to figure I had to be careful with any information I read. However, the thirty-third degree mason part led me to think he was probably not as orthodox as I am.

Now please do not think I have a vendetta against the Freemasons. Roman Catholics are excommunicated if they join the Freemasons. Please do not tell me "Father So and So said it was *okay*." The Vatican is very clear that it has not, is not, and will not be allowed. If Father so-and-so is your pastor, then you might want to question what else he might have wrong. In my life, I have had an opportunity to speak to two 33 degree Freemasons. Of course, they could not tell me anything significant, but it was very clear that they see the freemasonry as a religious organization. The lower levels are more public service oriented, like Shriner's Hospitals, and the Shriner's are riding their little motorcycles in the Fourth of July parade.

Rev. Dr. Paige was a 33 degree mason (that is as high as you can go folks), master of several lodges, general manager of the Grand Lodge, and on the Council overseeing the 33 degree masons. Do not let me forget he was the commissioner of the Knight Templar. There was no mention of the Illuminati, but maybe, they ran out of space. The *History Channel* could do a couple of shows on him. I am very knowledgeable in this area, and I have been interested in learning as much as I could about this subject for the past forty years. However, just like going to mediums, joining in their practices is strictly off-limits in my worldview.

I am back into some theological issues, but I guess I need to explain that I do believe in generational curses. In other words, if I involve myself in forbidden practices, I can bring down a negative consequences on myself and on my offspring down to the third and fourth generation, and there are Bible references to support this (Exodus 20:5, 34:7; Numbers 14:18; Deuteronomy 5:9). It is not so much that God is like this vengeful being waiting to whack us. Sin, like eye color, gets passed along. For example, if I am brought up in a household where my dad was running illegal betting for horses, I would probably see that as acceptable behavior. (Not that I have any firsthand experience, mind you, but the example just dropped on me, again.) Do you think that Rev. Dr.'s family was also involved in the Freemasons? My father never mentioned, it but that does not mean he did not know. One thing I learned from 33 degree masons: "Mum's the word."

I spent this morning saying some prayers and asking for prayer to break that curse. I know this works because, years ago, I saw alcoholism coming at me and my children from both sides of the family. I spent serious prayer time asking for them to be spared. It did go around my three children, but my brother's children were not so blessed. Some would claim it was my attitude rather than prayer that made the difference here, but I do have some real experience with this, and prayer works. At any rate, this was not something I was happy to learn about my ancestors, but I do believe forewarned was forearmed. It is better to know the enemy because you have a better idea about what defenses and weapons work best. For example, if you know you are fighting fire, it is not good to be near gasoline.

At any rate, this is not why I am writing this chapter; this is just the backstory. On the bottom of the page, about Rev. Dr. Paige, was one word that electrified me: *Mayflower*. I really thought that going back to the DAR was the be all and end all for me, so when I first saw it, I dismissed it. It kept nagging at me, however, but I only had a part of it of the description, like only having half the treasure map. It was clear that they were making a connection between Rev. Dr. Paige and someone who came over on the *Mayflower*. He was identified as a "direct descendant of Elder William Brewster." If Rev. Dr. Paige was a direct descendant of Elder Brewster, then so was I!

The more I dug, the more I was hooked on this quest. Elder Willian Brewster was a very well-known passenger on the *Mayflower* in 1620, and he was believed to be the author as well as a signatory of the Mayflower Compact. However, the description I had used antiquated language and abbreviations. There were too many people named Mercy, three to be exact, and John Freeman had eleven children that I could count. In addition, you would think folks on an ancestry site would be showing this connection all over the place, but many of the family timelines were not available. I could find them in a search, but the content was available only with the permission of the author(s). Of course, after all the problems I have had with these timelines, maybe, I should be just as happy I did not have to sift the wheat from the chaff.

I had to write it all down step-by-step. So first, I wrote down the name of Elder Brewster and his wife Mary. (Just what I need, more Marys; it is my middle name, and the Paige line is loaded with them.) They had a daughter, Patience, who married Governor Thomas Prince (or Prence). Patience and Thomas had a daughter, Mercy, who married John Freeman Sr. Mercy and John Sr. had John Freeman Jr. John Jr. had two wives, and the second wife was named Mercy, but all the children were from his first wife Sarah. Sarah was the mother of his eleven children, one of whom was named Mercy. Mercy Freeman married Chillingworth Foster, and they had a son, James Foster. James married Lydia Winslow. James and Lydia had a daughter, Mary Foster, who married Colonel Timothy Paige.

Now this simple paragraph represents about three hours of research, and I had to admit as I got to the end, my hands were shaking. I had papers all over the place that I had to clean up when I was done typing. I had to remind myself that if I was not a descendant of Elder Brewster, there was no loss because what I had was remarkable. But who would ever guess that I was going to discover the *Mayflower* as part of my past? This was an interesting discovery because I had no one significant to tell. I was not on a desert island, so there were living, breathing, sentient beings around but not ones who would appreciate this news.

The next day, I did write a memo to family members about this event. I have a very rudimentary family chart so that they could see I was not letting the DAR create delusions and included it with my memo. The thought of talking to each of them as individuals was overwhelming. I am not talking hundreds of individuals. I sent the memo to (a) my two brothers, (b) my three children, (c) two nieces, (d) my nephew, and (e) Marcia. If I am a descendant of Elder William Brewster, so is she.

I looked up the General Society of *Mayflower* Descendants. If you did not see this coming, you have not been paying attention. I have no plans to begin that process until the DAR membership is settled. I had two reasons for this: First, I do not want to try to do both things at the same time. Second, when the DAR accepts my genealogical evidence, I am hoping I can build on that for the *Mayflower* group. Third (see you were paying attention), I have other things to do, like my job, and this whole search and writing this memoir have taken plenty of time.

I do wonder how much further back I can go, Moses maybe?

Chapter 12

MR. BIG STUFF

> Now because you wear all those fancy clothes
> And have a big fine car, oh yes you do now
> Do you think I can afford to give you my love
> You think you're higher than every star above
> Mr. Big Stuff
> Who do you think you are
> Mr. Big Stuff
> You're never gonna get my love
> (Ralph Williams, Carrol Washington, Joseph Boussard [1970])

It has been a week since I wrote, and I have come to realize that these huge family discoveries are similar to the perfect high addicts which chase all through their substance-using and sober lives. There is a real high associated with the kind of discoveries I have made. I realized I could have also used the song "Is That All There Is?" for this chapter, but I did want to diminish all my discoveries. So I found a way to have vicarious discoveries.

The TLC network has a show entitled *Who Do You Think That You Are?* In each episode, a different celebrity goes on a journey to trace parts of his or her family tree (Wikipedia). I binge-watched; okay, five hours is a binge for me, yesterday. The day was also significant because it was the anniversary of my dad's passing.

One of the persons on the show was doing genealogical research in Pennsylvania, and I could relate to that. One person had a relative who was hanged at the Salem witch trials, and I realized how incredible my good luck was. There was some tragedy in my own search, like my stillborn Uncle John, but considering how tragic events in life really seems to outnumber the positive events, I felt like I had hit the ancestral lottery. There was another person who discovered they had a relative who was in the Revolutionary War, and they went to Washington, DC, to the DAR headquarters. I had tears in my eyes.

The link to the song lyric is obvious because of the line "Who do you think you are?" which is also the title of the show. There is another level of this soundtrack selection, however, that goes much deeper. I have really learned that the public does not necessarily care about their own relatives let alone mine. My friend Jane, who is DAR eligible, gets it. Outside of the note I sent to family members about our relationship with Elder William Brewster, Jane, and my DAR representative, I have not really told other folks about my genealogical discoveries.

From a vain perspective, part of me wants to have someone else verify the connection so I do not embarrass myself. The other part of me sees people looking at the connection as a type of braggadocio on my part. It has been a week, and the only family response I had was from my son and daughter, so I am not sure even they care about all this. I did mention it briefly to a colleague, and their response was somewhat in the vein of asking me if I was changing my social class. Please do not get me wrong. I am just as happy about my discoveries today as I was when I made the discovery, and I am the same person (but might I ask, Am I really?). What I have realized about myself is I am more in tune with cues from others. About ten years ago, I would have told anyone who was breathing about my discovery, but now, I am more restrained in my disclosures, and I think this is growth.

Part of this restraint may come from the catharsis of writing this memoir. The writing is giving me a chance to process all my discoveries and begin to think differently about my new reality. For example, another memory these discoveries prompted was a comment my mother used often in referring to my dad as a shanty Irishman. That term was not intended as a compliment, and because she identified me so closely with Dad, I am just like him; after all, her comments included me. Of course, her comments about Dad prompted me to wrap myself in green and professed myself as coming from the old sod.

Remember, my mother was intimidated by people with status, so maybe that was her own fear speaking about something in us she did not understand. She could see these characteristics in us, so she could not understand us. However, I saw the reference as pejorative because, to me, my mother's use of that term meant the same as "white trash." She went beyond a simple misunderstanding on her part, especially when directed at family members. Her family has strong positive characteristics as I alluded to in prior chapters. I believe she saw anyone who deviated from those standards as less worthy in her eyes.

The irony here is on two levels. Since I have discovered the connection to Elder Brewster, I remembered her scornful attitude about Dad's family and how we did not measure up. Nothing could be further from the truth when you view this history from a broader perspective. (Yes, that was a backhanded way of calling her narrow-minded.) As I have already written, I think I am fearful that, somehow, I have made a mistake in my research, and someone is going to tell me I was wrong and, worse, that she was right. The warm wonder I have had since I made the discovery would be a great loss to me. Remember how upset I was when I found the inaccurate timelines? This loss would be of a similar magnitude times ten.

The second irony is quite amusing. The idea that Dad was Irish and, by extension, that I am Irish does not appear too likely. From what I see in our genealogy, we are *hail Britannia* all the way. In fact, I have been spending some time thinking about what Elder William Brewster thinks of me—the practicing Roman Catholic—in his familial line. By the way, I am sure there are other besides me, so my musings are not too egocentric.

On one hand, Willian Brewster would have seen Catholics experience the same oppression in England that he did and, in some cases, worse than he experienced. He was alive and living in exile in

Holland for his religious practices when Guy Fawkes, a Catholic, was caught red-handed trying to blow up the same King James I who he had escaped. On the other hand, I believe, like my mother, William Brewster has had his perspective broadened once he crossed over into the next realm, so I think he will be happy to meet me one day. Frankly, I can find no Irish influence in the family line even in the spouses of the Paige men. One of the questions I must ask Dad when we next meet is if his Irish persona was a genuine mistake or a calculated theater on his part?

One of the things I learned from my binge-watching of TLC is that the people making discoveries on the show were as excited and elated as I was when they made discoveries about their families. One of the seekers discovered that an ancestor who was in the Revolutionary Army was a lifeguard. That does not mean he was guarding the Delaware River when Washington crossed. The term meant that he was selected to be in the first guard unit to protect George Washington. The man on the show was moved to discover that his ancestor had such an important role with our first president. I shed tears right along with him because I knew we were sharing the wonder and pride of such a discovery, and it was incredible. In my case, Elder Brewster was not just a passenger on the *Mayflower*, he was a leader and a religious one at that.

One other thing I should remind you about at this juncture is that this day was the anniversary of Dad's passing. I spent this day, as I always do on his anniversary date, thinking about and missing my dad. I did not have the answer to whether Dad knew about his linage before he died, but I was sure he knew it now. I could not help but wonder how he was getting along with all of them now.

For my part, I feel even more connected to the fate of this country than I did before. I have always voted and kept myself informed—actually I am a news junkie—about the running of my country. Dad used to say that if you did not vote, you could not bitch about how things were going in the country. Your vote was your ticket to bitch. My discoveries lead me to ponder a "chicken or the egg" reflection. Were these patriotic proclivities a reflection of my lineage? I may never know the answer to this question, but I do know these behaviors have been enhanced by all of this. My daughter Amanda suggested I should get a *Mayflower* tattoo, but I really need to take this under advisement.

Initially, I had intended to wait with looking into an organization for *Mayflower* descendants until after I had completed the DAR process. That scheme lasted for a short duration because I was getting restless, so I thought, *What the heck*! I went back to the Society of Mayflower Descendants and discovered the process was different than the DAR process. I could submit a tentative genealogy online so they could ascertain my prospects for membership. Of course, there was a fee to do this, but it was not prohibitive, so I submitted my lineage. As soon as I made the payment arrangements and hit the submit button, I knew I made a mistake; I skipped the generation connecting the Brewster line to the Paige line.

If I am going to make a mistake, it might as well be a big one, and to my mind, this was a big one. Do I pay the minimal fee again? The fee would not be so minimal if I paid it twice. I decided to send an email to the society asking if I needed to formally submit a corrected lineage. I put the corrected lineage in the email and told them I was in the process of applying for a DAR membership. The representative was quite prompt and told me I did not need to resubmit. Oh, happy day! It will take about two to four weeks for a response, so at least, that process has begun.

I am going to make a small confession here—remember Catholic guilt? When I send my yearly Christmas newsletter, I wanted to write about my membership in both groups, I hope. If I begin this process now, it might be a *fait accompli* by November. Now I know I wrote in this chapter that I was being selective with my audience for revealing my discoveries. However, Christmas newsletters are all about braggadocio, so that is a good way to announce the news. Besides, I will not see the smirks or hear the snide comments as they read the newsletter, so this really works for me.

One other occurrence of this week involves me and an inaccurate timeline on a genealogy website. These timelines were not about my Paige relatives or the Brewster family but my mother's Polish family. Now I ask you, if my experience with inaccurate information is not unusual on genealogy websites, then there is a great deal of misinformation on these sites. When it came to my mother's family, I knew these folks; I spoke with them, and I tend their grave sites as I wrote in the first chapter.

I was again prompted by some guilt because I had spent so much time researching my dad's family. I knew and loved my mother's Polish family, but I could only go back two generations, and even then, the information was sketchy. I did get my grandfather Adam's death certificate some time ago just to learn when he really died and the names of his parents. He was an immigrant from Russia or Poland depending on which document you were reading. I was always confused by this muddle about his country of origin. Then I saw a documentary on TV about the history of the Jews. I will come back to this in a minute. Poland was constantly changing governments, and Russia was one of the most notable conquering countries. Ethnically, he may have been Polish, but he could also have been Russian or Ukrainian.

Unlike Dad's family, I had more personal knowledge of my mother's family. My Uncle Harry, my mother's brother, told me a story about Adam while we were sitting at a poolside on a summer afternoon in my mother's backyard. I include these details because I want you to know the impact this story had on me. I remember the day some thirty years ago with such clarity it could have been yesterday.

He told me Adam and his two brothers, Stanley and Joseph, were taken from their home as teenagers and impressed into a Cossack Brigade of the Russian Army. This was pre-1917 and the revolution, so they were part of the czar's army. The three brothers were armor bearers with a gruesome task. The Cossacks held a wager over who would kill the most enemy soldiers in a battle. The three boys followed their Cossack soldier around the battlefield carrying a sack and collecting the heads of their vanquished enemy. At the end of the day, the sacks were emptied, and the skulls were counted to determine who won the wager. I am sure there were other circumstances, but Adam allowed alcohol and brooding to end his life in 1931 when my mother was nine years old.

Remember the reaction of my mother when I asked about a mafia connection to Pappy? Well, I got that reaction from her one other time. I innocently asked if she thought we might have Jewish blood. I knew many Jews converted to Christianity to avoid the pogroms in Russia and thought it was possible her father did the same. I have always been a Zionist, a Gentile one but a Zionist just the same. I liked the idea of being of Jewish descent but my mother not so much. She was horrified and angry at the suggestion, so needless to say, I kept these musings to myself, but I never stopped thinking about it. I do not want to appear greedy, but could we be descendants of Grand Duchess Anastasia Nikolaevna of the Romanova family? We share the same birth date on June 18. I suppose not, but I could not resist putting it in this narrative because I am still chasing the perfect high.

Back to the timelines. I found two timelines that had real errors about Adam's family, and I did not recognize either of the family names attached to the timelines. What the heck! I have spent so much time working my way through the Paige family and trying to make my best guess about who, what, where, and when. Now, I was looking at inaccurate information about family that I do know who, what, where, and when. You know what I did, right? You betcha. I sent emails to both families. I introduced myself as Adam's oldest grandchild and tried to inform them of the error of their ways.

One timeline author responded quickly to me. He wrote that he had taken information from the other site I had contacted. He had gone back to look at the areas I questioned, and he realized he was incorrect. He had taken information from the other site at face value, but now he knew better. He is also a relative of my aunt's first husband who died shortly after they were married, so at least, I knew his connection to Adam's family. No, we are not *the Addams' Family*. The other miscreants have yet to contact me. Their site even has a picture of my uncle's wedding, so I am real interested in who they are.

Let this be a lesson to all. Just because someone has posted *documented* information on a website, it does not mean the information is righteous. Nor does it mean that the authors' of said sites will welcome the virtuous individual who only wants to show them the errors of their ways. Maybe, I am starting to sound a little like Ms. Big Stuff. Who do I think I am? I am tempted to brag a little, but instead, I will just bide my time. Booker T. Washington once said that if a person is right, they should remain silent after they present their claims because if they are right, time will present them as such. So for a while, I will be silent.

Chapter 13

ANTICIPATION

> We can never know about the days to come
> But we think about them anyway
> And I wonder if I'm really with you now
> Or just chasing after some finer day.
> Anticipation, Anticipation
> Is making me late
> Is keeping me waiting
> (Carly Simon [1971], Anticipation)

Have you ever had an experience that surpassed your expectations? If you have had more of those experiences than the soul-crushing disappointment of having a greatly anticipated event fall flat, consider yourself lucky. I would say that about 1 percent of my experiences are of the former while the great majority are of the latter ilk. This happens often enough that I really try to reign in my expectations to try to avoid the disappointment. The best metaphor I can think of to describe this mental preparation is to compare it to using the brakes in my car. When an unexpected obstacle comes into view, I slow my speed to avoid or at least lessen the impact by putting my foot on the brake. I use mental brakes to try and slow down my anticipation and not build up expectations that can never be met. (I think you are beginning to see why the lyric for this chapter is "Anticipation" by Carly Simon.)

Now there is some wisdom in my approach. I settle down the manic part of my personality with my mental brakes. I like to think of myself as a passionate woman who cares deeply about the things I care deeply about. However, I cannot sustain that level of interest without exhausting myself and botching up the things I need to do that are right in front of me. There is a balance to maintain if I am to continue toward my goal. Sometimes, I apply the mental brakes too much and come to a halt short of my destination. Then the anticipated event suddenly seems to become more trouble than it is worth, and I let lethargy take the place of momentum and *anticipation*.

Now I suppose you are thinking, *Where is she going with this*? That is a very good question and shows me you are paying attention. It has been about a month since I sat down to work on this memoir, and a few things have occurred. I will begin by telling you that there have been *no* new ancestry discoveries like my mother being a direct descendant of Moses. (I know in the last chapter, I suggested the royal family of the Russian Czar, but remember my musings about Jewish ancestry?) That would, of course, be nice, but I also know I should not get greedy. Other members of mankind should have access to the great ones. (Did you feel me tapping the brakes?)

Besides, I had work to do. The semester has ended, and there are the final grades to calculate, end of the year meetings and report, and weeds in my garden (it is spring now) that mock me every day I leave them unmolested. I am also working on another book with colleagues about academic interests, and that is now clamoring for my attention, and yet here I am with my two fingers typing away at this memoir. Where are my priorities? I guess my behavior makes that very clear.

In between the above activities, I looked daily for a response from the Genealogical Society of Mayflower Descendants. True to their word, it took about three to four weeks for them to respond to my inquiry, but it was worth the wait. They wrote,

> Then GS#—— matches your proposed lineage from Mayflower passenger William Brewster through the new 7th generation: Mary Foster M. Timothy Paige. This is a well-documented paper,

> which then follows this couple's son, Moses Paige, apparently a brother of Timothy Paige. An older and less well documented paper, GS#——— continues your line through the 10th generation marriage of Timothy Paige and Rebecca Richardson. This paper then follows Edwin Paige, presumably a brother of your great-grandfather, George Paige. This older paper is not up-to-date but may provide some useful information and guidance. (Personal Communication; May 14, 2016)

By now, some of these names are meaningful to you, so you can imagine my glee as I read their evaluation.

Now in my brake-tapping mentality, I had preplanned to complete DAR before I began this journey, *but* I could not come up with a good reason why I needed to do this. Formal application to the Society of Mayflower Descendants must be made through state affiliates. I got busy getting my application together and sending them yet another non-refundable check to begin the work with their genealogical historian. My check cleared today, so at least, we are moving forward, and yet again, I tap the brakes.

I want to interject one other side-effect of this search. My ten-year-old grandson Brayden, son of my son, would not be affected by the DAR material but he is with the Society of Mayflower Descendants. He told me he went to school to tell his social studies teacher about his newly discovered *Mayflower* ancestor. I was able to tell him more about William Brewster, and he was really enthused to learn more about the history and the time all this occurred. We are approaching the four hundredth anniversary of the Pilgrim landing at Plymouth in 1620, and I know Brayden will be interested is this event. In addition, I know Thanksgiving will never be the same for my family because we had a guy at the table.

The event that really prompted this chapter, however, was my first DAR meeting. In all honesty, when the night came, I was not even feeling like attending. Remember, I wrote that sometimes my break-tapping can lead to a complete stop, and this was such an event. As I get older, going to new places and beginning new things is not as readily embraced either, so this was in play as well. But I made it. I found the location, and my DAR representative saw me coming and met me at the door to show me to the meeting room. That was one of my nagging thoughts, *How will I find the room once I find the location*? Once again, I fretted for nothing.

There were about twelve women in the room, and three of us were there for the first time. I sat next to my DAR rep, and she walked me through the meeting. The meeting room and its occupants were welcoming, so I was at ease as we began the opening ceremony. I will not detail the exact content, and no, I did not take a blood oath to keep it secret, but the opening rite contained two scripture verses and the pledge of allegiance. Now, if you have read this memoir, you will know that I was so choked up I could barely contain my tears. My Christian beliefs and my love of country and the military were combined in one simple invocation. These words and actions reached into a greater depth of my being than I thought possible. All I could think of was, *This group was made for me*! and *Where were they all my life*?

During the meeting, as community service, I wrote a letter to a member of the military thanking him or her for their service to the country. The regent for the affiliate spoke about attending citizenship ceremonies to pass out American flags to new citizens. There were discussions about other services that the DAR performs and planning for future activities. If that was not enough, I then watched my DAR rep have the members sign my formal application to send to Washington, DC, for final approval. I could hardly contain myself, *but* there was one small document that would delay the forwarding of my application. Just when I was accelerating toward my goal, I had to slam on the brakes.

Irony of ironies, it was documentation from my mother and on my mother. The first issue was my father's death certificate that listed his mother's name as Emma O'Hara. Of course, that is not his mother's name; Emma was his mother. However, that did not match the information given by my mother on my father's death certificate. Did you ever try to explain to someone why a wife did not know the name of her own mother-in-law? You have read this, so I know you know why. Truth be told, it has nagged me that when my paperwork got to Washington, this was going to be flagged as a problem, and sure enough, there it was. The only difference was it got flagged here.

Second, the DAR is fussy about the documentation on the first three generations. I was not as concerned about my mother because it was not her line I was following for membership, but the DAR has other thoughts. So now, I must get her death certificate. This is about, I hope, at least a two-week wait while I send the request and wait for a civil servant to dig up her death certificate, make me a copy, and send it through snail mail. Can you hear my brakes screeching? Smell the rubber burning? No kidding, I could almost feel my mother's smirk as I found out what I needed to do to get her death certificate. This activity included but was not limited to getting a $10 money order that cost me $5, a notarized signature, getting the request into the mail, and waiting.

Years ago, there was a ketchup commercial that use "Anticipation" as the background music and lyric. As you waited for their wonderful product came out of the bottle and on to a hamburger, you heard Carly Simon sing those familiar lyrics. She is singing to me now, in my head, as I type these words. I am trying to convince myself that that there is a good reason for this delay and that things will work themselves out for the best. But when my mother is involved, it is difficult to avoid the sinking feeling that there is mischief afoot.

I know I am giving her too much power, but the thought that keeps creeping into my head is that she did this on purpose in 1977 to mess up my plans some forty years later. I know if she were alive today, she would not be happy about my discoveries. Remember, I had to get Dad's military records on the sly, and I would still be doing this research today, behind her back, if she were alive. I could counter her by reminding her that Memorial Day is this weekend, and I am the keeper of the graves. Yet she trumps me again. She is buried in a mausoleum that need no grass to be trimmed and/or flowers planted. You only read about the woman, but I knew her and lived with her, and I learned early *never* to underestimate her. Of course, you might think that I am somewhat paranoid. I would counter with you are only paranoid if you are wrong!

Chapter 14

I'M SORRY

> You tell me mistakes
> Are part of being young
> But that don't right
> The wrong that's been done
> (I'm sorry) I'm sorry
> (So sorry) So sorry
> Please accept my apology
> But love is blind
> And I was too blind to see
> (I'm Sorry [1960] Dub Allbritten and Ronnie
>   Shelf)

You, young ones, may not know this song lyric. If you do not know this tune, go online and listen to the words and melody sung by fifteen-year-old Brenda Lee. I know it refers to being "young." I am young at heart, so I can take some license with the application to my soundtrack. As you read on, you will understand my apology not only to you but also to my mother and civil servants everywhere.

    I had just completed the words at the end of the last chapter, gone home, and in the mailbox was my mother's death certificate. My subtle stab at civil servants was completely uncalled for this time. In addition, my mother was not stalling my DAR application very much. I had the copies made and in the mail to my DAR rep the next day. I immediately considered revising the end of the last chapter, but I did not do it for two reasons.

First, I have made no secret that I am a Catholic. Many folks are familiar with the term "Catholic guilt." When the term is applied to an individual, it is usually a pejorative. I take it in quite the opposite meaning however. I think honesty is the best approach to life. As I share my humanity with others, it reminds me that all of us have a turn at difficulty. Sometimes, we handle it well, but sometimes, we let bias and impatience cloud our judgment, and the self we expose is not so appealing. I think we all need to achieve a balance in life, and so it was consistent with my personal beliefs to begin this chapter by identifying my rash judgments and offering an apology. I am a bit paranoid, and I had a less than wonderful relationship with my mother. None of this is an excuse for harsh conclusions.

Second, I made it very clear from the onset that this memoir is in the form of a journal. If I wish to write with that perspective, it is right for me to share my frustrations and impatience as they occur *and* acknowledge the same to you, the reader. I want you to share in the emotions involved in my search for family. I should also add the increasingly expensive venture that is a genealogy search. Now, if I ever get lucky enough to have someone actually publish this memoir, then you can help in that aspect of this journey.

So this chapter deals with my hectic activity in the past forty-eight hours. You know about the timely arrival of the death certificate. When I went to work the next morning, I had an email from the Society of Mayflower Descendants. The *very* good news was that, Sarah, the historian working with my application, was able to trace from William Brewster all the way to Great-Granddad George. She needed only partial information for his line on the genealogy and some information on Great-Grandmother Louisa. I only needed full information (birth, death, marriage) for the last three generations: Pappy and Emma, Dad and Mom, and me.

I did send an email to Sarah about my mother's error on my father's death certificate (Nancy O'Hara as Dad's mother). She responded that there was no problem with this because they request so much supporting evidence that errors can be identified. *Mea culpa.* This is a little Latin Catholic lingo, taken from the opening penitential prayer at the beginning of Mass, which has made it into the lexicon. The basic interpretation is I'm sorry. I did need a notarized letter requesting my mother's birth certificate (cha-ching) along with her death certificate that I just received. Finding a notary is a pain for me because I am a notary, but that is of no use in notarizing my own signature. So I was printing, making copies, writing a letter, going to the bank for the notary, and, of course, the post office all before lunch.

Now lunch was interesting. I was meeting with two other women who were up to their lovely armpits in genealogy. My friend had asked me what was going on with my search. I have already written over thirty thousand words about this subject, so where do I start? I suggested a lunch where we could catch up, and I could try to encapsulate my activity. I have a very bad habit of getting caught up in minutia, so I had to ponder how to summarize all this. I came on what I thought was the perfect solution to summarizing what had been going on with my search.

Sarah had sent me a lovely three-page outline of my line beginning with William Brewster on the society letterhead. I was very patient waiting to show them my discoveries. When I was asked what I had discovered, after lunch was finished, I replied that I thought it was best to start at the end of the story. So I brought out Sarah's letter. I will not go into exactly what was said, but suffice it to say, the letter was back in my purse in less than two minutes.

I have addressed my reluctance in telling folks about all of this. I really thought I had found the perfect persons to reveal my great discoveries. Without going into detail about what was said, which was not much, it is easier to say what was not said. The comments were more about "not in my family" and little or no interest about the DAR or the Society of Mayflower Descendants. I was surprised and not surprised. I understood this was a common response, but I did not expect it in this situation. It has not dampened my enthusiasm, but I do need to ponder what is going on here. I will get back to you on this one.

One other thing I noticed is the chill that seems to exist between the DAR and the Society. I had written previously that I had emailed my DAR rep about the discovery of William Brewster and looking into the Society. The email was not acknowledged at the time; however, she did make a reference to "that other group" at the meeting. I was struck by the vagueness of the comment. It was like how people use euphuisms to refer to someone or something that should not be mentioned.

I had informed the Society that I was in the process of joining the DAR, and I had no direct response to this revelation. However, in their paperwork, the Society is quite clear that DAR searches have no relevance in their work. The Pilgrims do not like the patriots? What is up with that? I now know to tread softly with this issue, but I intend to get to the bottom of it. Stay tuned!

To fill out the past forty-eight hours, I thought, while I was spending money, I might as well get the DNA test done. Unless you are living in a refrigerator box in Montana, you have seen or heard the media advertising this service. Some guy exchanged his lederhosen (German) for a kilt (Scotland) when he received his DNA results. I do not anticipate such a radical response; however, I will be interested to know if there is Jewish markers in my report.

The idea came up at lunch, and one of the lovely ladies sent me an online link for the test at a reduced rate. Basically, I will be sent a kit to swab the inside of my mouth. Once that is done, I put the swab in a postpaid package, give it to the mailman, and wait for an email. I got the deluxe version, so my DNA is compared to *all* the continents. My paranoia had kept me away from this test because I could see "big brother" getting my DNA to put in a database. They already have my fingerprints because it is part of my teaching license process, so I figured why not?

I am tired just trying to write all of this down. I was thinking about this the other day. If I had not begum writing when I did, a great deal of the story would be lost. I have been through so many changes during this process that I would not have recalled all the ebb and flow of this journey. In addition, the process of writing this all down has helped me sort through so many of the events and emotions of my life and how they relate to one another. For example, my story about the scene on TV about the Musicorps that caused tears from such a deep place. This event helped me to cope with the loss of Texas, Val my protector dog, and my "military guard" at Fort Sam.

When I was collecting the documentation for the Society, I was struck by the dates on the correspondence about the documents I had amassed going back to the turn of the century. I need all of those documents now, but it took me years to collect it and more years to organize and begin to make sense of this mass of data. For so long, I kept hitting a brick wall, and then, one brick at a time, information was revealed, and soon, so many things I thought I knew changed. For the most part, the change was for the better. Some of the death and sadness I encountered also made me more aware of the chaos that proceeded my lifetime. I guess this also brings me to my song theme for this chapter. I can truly say "I'm sorry" to the folks in the cloud for the early loss of parents, loss of innocence, and loss of identity and connection with family.

Chapter 15

MY EYES ADORED YOU

My eyes adored you
Though I never laid a hand on you
My eyes adored you
Like a million miles away
From me you couldn't see
How I adored you
So close, so close
And yet so far away
(Bob Crewe and Kenny Nolan [1971] performed
    by Frankie Vallie)

On Wikipedia, I learned that this song had some difficulty finding a performer and a record label back in 1971. Fortunately, for me and you, it did find both and remains a well-known standard love song even today. Of course, this song is about an individual who longs for the attention and companionship of a beloved person. Before you begin to wonder, I am not interested in another husband, been there and done that. I am writing about my love affair with two organizations: the Daughters of the American Revolution (DAR) and the General Society of Mayflower Descendants (GSMD). In the month since I last wrote, I have attended my second DAR meeting and communicated with GSMD.

My second *date* with the DAR left me falling harder and harder for this beloved. It was a June Saturday luncheon meeting at a member's home. There are no regular meetings in July and August, so this was a send-off for the summer and an opportunity to go over other DAR organizational issues that occur during the summer months. I carpooled with Donna for the thirty-minute ride, and we had a chance to talk about my paperwork. She was sending it into the national office this week, and she had found some new information to add to my file; more on this later. Since the last meeting, I had ordered my mother's birth certificate, received it, and sent Donna a copy to add to my record. She was confident she had enough without Pappy and Emma's marriage license, but more on this later as well.

The opening ceremony still gave me goosebumps because the scripture reference, pledge of allegiance, and talk of patriotism and country resonated to the depth of my being. Now if you have read this whole memoir, and paid attention, you can begin to understand why this happened. The meeting proceeded with the usual business that most organizations deal with: minutes, treasurer's repost, correspondence membership, etc. It is here that I need to interject what I was thinking.

When I attend most meetings, I pay attention, check off the agenda items, and hope the meeting ends on time. In addition, I make myself small when the subject of volunteers for committees, fundraisers, and the like arise. At this meeting, I surprised myself because I was thinking "I could do that!" more than once. As a visiting member, at this point, I can only sit and listen, but my desire to be involved surprised me most of all.

When the business of the meeting ended, I had a chance to chat with some of the members over lunch. I am sure my enthusiasm for DAR was quite apparent to them because they asked me to write down full contact information before I left. Like many organizations, their membership rolls far surpass their attendance; they had fifty members enrolled and only seven persons counting me at this meeting. This summer break might be just the thing I need to have my credentials evaluated and approved. To be on the safe side, I ended every statement with "…when my membership is approved."

This was also an opportunity to learn more about DAR. This list is in no order of priority but a compilation of membership details:

1. There is an induction program once approval is obtained from the national group.
2. All members have a membership number assigned.
3. There are pins and ribbons that members wear and only at DAR events. There are add-ons to the basic membership pin for service to DAR, serving as an officer, supplemental membership, etc. Once applications are approved, I will receive a book with all my options, and apparently, I can spend as much as my budget will allow.
4. I can put a DAR logo on my tombstone! Why the exclamation point? I just finished paying for my cemetery plots so these plans are fresh on my mind.
5. I can have a supplemental membership because the captain is in my line as well as the colonel. Can you believe I am making such plans already? September seems so far away, but the reality is the timing is perfect. The members are welcoming, and I feel so comfortable with them I hated to see the meeting end.

I also have a partial answer to the chill I perceived between DAR and GSMD that I speculated on in a prior chapter. I was very surprised at the meeting when another member mentioned GSMD. She had discovered the connection to the *Mayflower* in her lineage, as I had, and was in the application process as I am. I spoke up that I was doing the same thing. She is a descendant of John Alden as I am of William Brewster. The NYS GSMD group meets twice a year; the next meeting is in November, and we might travel together to the meeting. I think the chill is simply a way to let members of one group know that membership in one of them is not automatic membership in the other. I was quite happy with my discovery that I had a connection to the GSMD.

THE SOUNDTRACK OF MY LIFE

I had submitted a check and application to GSMD over a month ago, and I received a reply about three weeks later. To my great joy and relief, they were able to verify the line down to Great-Grandfather George. I could not believe it could be this easy (and I was right because it was not). I needed Great-Grandfather George's death certificate and the documents (birth, death, marriage) for Pappy and Emma, Mom and Dad, and me.

I was concerned about not being able to find a marriage license for Pappy and Emma. I do not have an exact count of how many hours and how many searches I made looking for this document, but it adds up to hours of computer time I wish I could have back. I did send an email to GSMD about my inability to locate the document, and the response I received indicated that they could use other supporting information. However, I did need Great-Grandfather George's death certificate so yet again another check to Rhode Island for yet another document.

I received an email several days ago that the work was almost done, and we would have to let the GSMD board make the decision on the supporting documentation I sent in lieu of the marriage certificate for Pappy and Emma. I have sent the birth certificates for Dad, Anne, John as well as Emma's death certificate—all listing Frank Paige as husband/father. (I ordered Emma's birth certificate today, just in case.) Because you are reading the fifteenth chapter of this book, you are aware of how easily I can see all my plans fall into dust and ashes. Yes, I am fighting off discouragement.

I will not rest until all of this is resolved and, of course, the certificates I ordered inform you that the waiting period is six to eight weeks. Now in my mother's case, I was pleasantly surprised by the efficiency of civil servants, but that was then, and this is now. However, all of this is out of my hands for the moment, and I will just have to do other things while I wait, like my job. It is not like any of this vision quest, *sans* a sweat lodge, has been easy; if it was, it would not be a vision quest, and why write a book? Look how many chapters I have written about all of this.

Two small but interesting things occurred this last month. First, I have written about the usual reaction ("Do I treat you differently now?") I get to my DAR and GSMD membership from friends. (By the way, I asked about this at the DAR meeting, and some had to admit that they did see it from time to time.) Well, I have some close colleagues at work, and we were sharing personal news with one another because we are close. When I told them about the DAR, a female colleague absolutely beamed at me, and I will never forget her reaction. I told her that she was among a very small minority and how much I appreciated her response. Maybe I have found a true friend detector in the DAR? I will have to study this further.

The second event was that I overcame my paranoia about privacy and sent a DNA swab in for ancestry analysis. As a licensed teacher, my fingerprints are already on record, and my garbage can is full of my DNA. I was told by a law enforcement agent that once we put the garbage on the curb, it becomes public property, so let that be a lesson to you. The thing that pushed me over the line was not the Paige family but my Polish-Russian Grandfather Adam and wondering if there is any indication of a Jewish heritage. Just for the record, I would be quite happy if there were.

The new information that Donna gave me was referenced in a book entitled *William Reade of Woburn and His Descendants.* My first reaction, why Reade? Then I remembered that the colonel's mother was Elizabeth Reade, and she was married to deacon Christopher Paige. The more I research, the more my family fills up with Protestant ministers; I wonder what they think of their Catholic descendant—more on this in the next chapter. I will just keep praying for them so they will be ready for me when we meet. The ultimate irony was that I discovered that my father was not the first Paige in his family to move to Dunkirk. My great, great-grandfather Martin had a sister named Mary Paige who married Colonel Thomas Wheeler. They had a daughter Rebecca Ann (1816–1853) who married Lyman Burrill of Dunkirk in 1837. I will have to do some research and find out if she was buried there. The family name is one I am not familiar with, but who knows what I will discover. Stay tuned.

Like the lyric says "…so close and yet so far away." It has taken some time to wrap my head around this new identity with the colonel and William Brewster as my ancestors. Now I have to entertain the possibility that I lack the proper credentials to join the DAR and GSMD. I think DAR is less in doubt, but one never knows until the judgment is rendered. Will I quit? Of course not, but I am weary of supporting the vital record bureaus in the Northeast US. Well, the jury is out, and now, there is nothing more to do but to wait for the verdict.

Chapter 16

HEY, YOU GET OFF OF MY CLOUD

> I said, "Hey, you, get off of my cloud
> Hey, you, get off of my cloud
> Hey, you, get off of my cloud
> Don't hang around cause two's a crowd
> On my cloud"
> Hey, you, get off of my cloud
> Hey, you, get off of my cloud
> Hey, you, get off of my cloud
> Don't hang around, baby two's a crowd
> On my cloud
> (Rolling Stones [1965] *December's Children (And Everybody's)*)

As I begin to write this chapter, I am not sure what it will contain. In the past, I had the chapter content in my head, and the music/song emerged as the chapter took form. In this case, the song lyric occurred to me first. Recently, I was driving my car and thinking about this book and the title of this Rolling Stone's tune came to mind, and it made me laugh out loud. For a mind like mine that loves metaphors, double *entendres* and/or alliterations (see *V for Vendetta*), it was lovely and appropriate. Why you ask? Let me count the ways.

I have already indicated that I believe the past generations of my family are deeply interested in my discoveries, and I call the place where they reside the (Paige) Cloud. I felt this was an accurate description of their habitation at several levels. First, Heaven is a common term to describe a part of the afterlife. For whatever reason, people often refer to its location in relation to our earthly domain as up where the clouds are. (That is, of course, opposite to the other aspect of the afterlife that is down below the earth.) How often are the inhabitants of Heaven portrayed floating on clouds, playing harps, and surrounded by angels? The literal view of the cloud as part of Heaven is widely held, so it is a reasonable place for my family.

Second, I do not think all my ancestors were saints. I believe they tended to be Christians who believe in the afterlife, and they purposely lead their lives to get to Heaven and avoid Hell. In addition, as a Roman Catholic—a religious affiliation that would not have the approval of my Paige and Brewster progenitors—I have tried to do my part with prayers and Masses for their souls to help them along in their journey to the (Paige) Cloud. (Remember, Purgatory is part of my belief system.) I believe that in the grand scheme, many of them were successful, and as they arrive in Heaven, they reunite as a group with other family members.

In chapter 1, I recounted my nocturnal visit by Grandma Emma, and I pondered what her cryptic (get the pun-crypt, cryptic?) request meant: "You need to bring the family together." Well, I think my genealogy search, prayers, and this book are doing just that. (Thank God, I no longer think moving graves is in my future.) I believe Elder Brewster, the colonel, the captain, Pappy, and Dad, among others, have a common place to gather, and I choose to call that place the (Paige) Cloud. Think of it as a heavenly subdivision of the cloud realm of Heaven.

Third, I recently found my reading matter to include Dante's "Divine Comedy" as translated by Burton Raffel (2010). If you are unfamiliar with this epic poem, then I will tell you it is about Dante's tour of the afterlife, Hell, Purgatory, and Heaven and his discussions with his guides and some of the inhabitants of each realm. Truth be told, Dante, like myself, is a Roman Catholic, so his views and my views about the hereafter are quite similar. What I found striking was that Dante's poem and this memoir are separated by seven hundred years, and yet the essence of our beliefs are mirror images.

When Dante reaches the first level of Heaven (paradise, Canto 2, ln. 31–36) he wrote,

> I felt that we were now inside a cloud—
> Bright, dense, solid, and polished clean,
> Like a diamond gleaming in the rays of the sun.
> This eternal pearl was open to us, receiving
> Our presence as water receives a shaft of light,
> Permitting this penetration which leaves it whole.

Now truth be told, the physical location of this first level is identified by Dante as the moon. I contend; though the moon is somewhat higher than our visible clouds, it is up. In addition, Dante is constantly missing many meanings in his afterlife tour because he is trying to understand a spiritual realm with his physical senses, and I believe I labor under the same difficulty. He thinks it is like a cloud, and so do I.

Fourth, unless you are living in a refrigerator box in northern Montana with a squirrel-powered generator, you are aware that all sorts of digital information are stored in the cloud. It has become a common term in the twenty-first century, and for me, it identifies where the collective history of my family is stored: in the souls of my deceased ancestors. Again, I refer to my dream of Grandma Emma, and I am coming to see her request in much broader terms and realizing that I do have some part to play bringing the family together. I am a practicing, Orthodox Roman Catholic, and in all my genealogy work, I am the only one of this particular spiritual persuasion in my direct line to the Paige, Farmer, and Brewster clans. I am coming to see this as very significant.

My brother is a Protestant minister, so he fits right in with our antecedents like William Brewster. For him prayers for the dead are unnecessary. I do not share his views, and I believe my prayers, Masses, and thoughts are a balm to the long dead. When they,

William Brewster and company, died, their Protestant brethren saw their passing as a *fait accompli*. As an elected/predestined individual, aka John Calvin, they were no longer in need of our prayers. In my worldview, clinging to that belief is like walking off the ledge of a ten-story building because you do not believe in gravity; believe in it or not, gravity will determine the outcome. You can believe in Purgatory or not, but your belief will not change your destination.

The Catechism of the Catholic Church declares, "Our prayer for them [the dead in Christ] is capable of not only helping them but also of making their intersession for us effective" (959). This citation is not an effort to turn this book into a sermon but rather to simply be accurate. As any good academic would do, I am simply going to the original sources. Far be it from me to lead my readers into error.

I believe my conviction about the efficacy of these prayers and Masses for the deceased has been enhanced because of Dante's "Divine Comedy." Imagine my surprise when I saw the new Dan Brown book-to-movie venture is *Inferno*. You guessed it—a new mystery to solve, and this one is embedded in "The Divine Comedy." Truth be told, I was required to read the first part, the *Inferno*, as an undergraduate college student in a literature class. (I will not write what the year was, but suffice it to say I was in college with Fred, Barney, and Wilma.) Believe it or not, Pope Francis suggested "The Divine Comedy" as a reading for this Year of Mercy, and I thought, *Why not?* I remember very little from my first encounter, but I am enjoying the reading, and I hate to put the book down.

Dante begins with the *Inferno*, and it is clearly Hell. (I have a few nominations for the last circle of Hell that Dante would not know about in 1320, but I digress.) In the *Inferno*, Dante travels down, down, down through the circles of Hell (and not all of them burning with fire and brimstone; some folks were frozen in ice) with the lowest level reserved for the worst of the unrepentant. When I read the second part, "Purgatorio," I was struck by the repeated pleas of the spirits to Dante to ask him and others for prayers. The souls who are in Purgatory cannot pray for themselves and are dependent on the living for their advancement to Heaven. Of course, Dante was a Catholic, and he would follow church teaching. (I should add similar requests are reported repeatedly by the living who were visited by the spirits of the dead asking for prayers and especially Masses. If this is of interest to you, check out the work of Susan Tassone.) I began to wonder if my ancestors were influential in this reading selection because it certainly increased my attention to their souls and the need for prayers on their behalf.

Purgatory separates Heaven and Hell. Let me be clear that in the Catholic view, someone cannot progress from Hell to Heaven through Purgatory. The *Catechism of the Catholic Church* is very clear that the suffering of the souls in Purgatory is very different from the suffering of the souls of the damned (1031). I like to think of Purgatory as a body shop for the soul. Like a car, a soul can pass inspection to enter Heaven, but some individuals may need to clean up (see burning wood, hay, and stubble in 1 Corinthians 3:12–15) like removing the dents, getting a new paint job, and a wash and wax to stand in the presence of God (1030). Dante portrays the souls in Purgatory as loving in this life, but their love was skewed by both extremes of the seven capital sins (being lustful or puritanical) and so the need for some "body" work.

When we want to impress and/or, for special occasions, we wash and shine the car, so in the natural realm, this concept is not new to us. Somehow, we do not think that God cares how we look, and for proof, just look around some contemporary church services. I think about the parable of the wedding guest without a proper wedding garment who was bound and thrown out into the darkness (Matthew 22:1–14). Jesus said the kingdom of Heaven is like this, so could it be any plainer to those who like literal interpretation? There is a famous hymn about how God accepts a sinner entitled, "Just As I Am." While that may be true, for that moment of grace and salvation, the reality is He is not going to leave us that way. At any rate, I believe prayers and/or Masses have brought the family together in the (Paige) Cloud.

Now the lyric of the song is demanding that "…you get off of my cloud…" so this is somewhat contrary to what you read about the souls of the elect who want to gather. However, I believe this lyric represents the antithesis of the condition of elect souls. The spirits in the *Inferno* want to be alone in their suffering and all the while declaring their innocence of any wrongdoing—in a word, narcissist. So Hell could easily be full of solitary and dreary clouds—dare I say fog? One thing that Dante repeatedly portrays in the *Inferno* is the unrepentant nature of the damned, be they pope, priest, noble, or pauper. These souls have no interest in my genealogy because in Hell, as on here on earth, they are all wrapped in themselves.

When I made discoveries about Pappy and Dad both losing their mothers at a young age and neither of them being raised by their fathers, I could only make a guess about how this pain formed the rest of their lives. I have been hearing so much data about the importance of fathers and father wounds and how the role of a father, even a bad father, is critical in the development of a man when he becomes a father and a woman when she selects a husband.

I know my dad was resentful of his father putting him in foster care when Emma died, but how much did he know about Pappy's past? I believe those hurts are now viewed by Dad and Pappy through the light of eternity and are now long forgotten. My dad and hence my family had some bad years with alcohol (remember the *Days of Wine and Roses*), yet I dedicated my dissertation to Dad because he was the light that kept me on the path to continue on with my education in spite of his weakness. My mother did not understand this, but even though my dad was dead, I was able to push on toward my goal because I had adopted his values about education.

One last point here is a reiteration of an argument I made in an earlier chapter. Even though Pappy died about fifteen months before I was born, I do not believe it is too late for me to pray for his soul. In this existence, we are stuck in a linear time frame of yesterday, today, and tomorrow. God has no such boundaries, and when our prayers reach Him, neither are they limited by the succession of days. William Brewster has been dead for over 350 years, yet I pray for him in ways I suspect no one else has. Otherwise, how could I bring the family together short of moving graves around? There are some mysteries I will need to carry to the (Paige) Cloud and ask them directly. Who raised Pappy? How did he get to Ohio? How did Pappy meet Emma? Where did they get married? I am looking forward to the homecoming, and I am sure no one will tell me to get off their cloud. I think they will be waiting for me.

Oh yes, this chapter should have a genealogical update. My understanding is that DAR has forwarded my paperwork to Washington, DC, for approval. GSMD sent me paperwork to sign for final submission for approval, *but* we must wait for Great-Granddad George's death certificate. That process was slowed down a bit because the state of Rhode Island returned my request because the Department of Health only has death records to 1965, and of course, he died in 1926. So I put more postage on yet another envelope and mailed the request back to the State Archives of Rhode Island. Did I mention these are both state agencies located in Providence? I guess they do not communicate with one another. I got my request for Emma's birth certificate returned as well because I sent it to the state, and I had to send it to the county. My advice to you, if you want to embark on a journey like mine, is put lots of money away for postage and certificates of birth, marriage, and death.

I began this chapter by writing that I did not know where I was going with my memoir. In looking over the words I have written, I surprised myself with the content, and I am not displeased. I have come to realize that the content of this chapter is a little more prosaic in that I deal with some philosophical and religious issues. Without the context of my worldview, many of my decisions would not make a great deal of sense to you, the reader. We, humans, can maintain interest in stories that are outside our experience but not so much for stories that ask the reader to suspend their intellect. It is not so important that you agree with me but rather that my decision-making is logical and consistent with my beliefs so you do not have to suspend reality to appreciate my story. After all, this is an autobiography, and I want you to join me. You do not have to get off of my cloud—the more, the merrier.

Chapter 17

SOMEWHERE MY LOVE

> There will be songs to sing
> Although the snow
> Covers the hope of spring
> Where are the beautiful days?
> Where are the sleigh rides to dawn?
> Where are the tender moments of splendor?
> Where have they gone, where have they gone?
> (Somewhere My Love [Lara's Theme] [1965],
>   Music Maurice Jarr and Lyrics Paul Francis
>   Webster)

The soundtrack for this chapter is the very famous "Lara's Theme" from the movie *Dr. Zhivago* (1965). For those of you who are too young to remember or for those of you who are old enough but still do not remember, this lovely melody owned the airwaves in 1965–66. If you have seen one of my favorite movies *Must Love Dogs*, the male lead, John Cusack, loved *Dr. Zhivago* and bemoaned a world that could not appreciate the Russian angst and suffering in the love story. When I think of Russia, I think of this piece of music, and as you read on, you will come to know why.

The other thing to remember as you read this chapter is this is a love song for a movie plot that has plenty of Russian angst. Some love stories are romantic and have a happy ending, and some end in tragedy like the story of Yuri Zhivago and the lovely Lara. Yuri already had a wife, and Lara had a husband, but their attraction to one another presents us with an irresistible passion while the protagonists try to do the right thing by their spouses. While I know the elements of this story are not an identical match to my grandparents' story, there is certainly many similarities including Cossack soldiers.

When I began this memoir, I was focused on the Paige side of my family. As I wrote in the previous chapter, my dreams are currently on hold as I wait for acceptance from the DAR and GSMD. It is said that "idle hands are the devil's workshop," and far be it from me to cooperate with the prince of darkness. In addition, I was feeling like I was ignoring my mother's family contribution to me, so I thought, *Why not look more closely while I had some time*?

My maternal grandmother, Mary, was the only grandparent I knew. She died when I was twelve years old, and I was old enough to have concrete memories of her. I was her first grandchild, and my middle name was her first name so that should have set us up for a lovely warm cookies and milk relationship, but that was not to be. I think the army has drill sergeants who were softer than she was. There were phrases she said to me over and over again, and they are the first things to come to mind when I think of her. They included but are not limited to, "Your generation will see the end of the world." "Why are you always making trouble for your mother?" "You need to take care of (fill in the blank) yourself because your mother has too much to do already." "Take care of your brother, Jim, and help your mother." If you notice the phrase, "I love you" or a reasonable facsimile is not included. For the first time in my life, as I type this with my two fingers, I cannot recall that she ever said it to me.

My mother would tell me, "You know she loves you because of the things she does for you." (We lived together, except for a two-year period, until she died.) That became the way love was to be distinguished in the family, and it made my father's absence in Europe even more difficult. My mother repeated this definition of love to me a great deal, but it did not soften my view of her, and I always tried to avoid her. If you recall in a past chapter, I described my arrival in Dunkirk with the snow on the ground and moving in with my grandmother, two uncles, and an aunt. I described them as strangers, and that contributed to my reticence about the move.

We all lived in a big old house that easily accommodated my mother, brother, and I along with the others. I remember there was no running water/sink in the kitchen when we first moved in, and it was a big event when running water was added. The living room and kitchen were both huge and had enormous plate glass picture windows because the house was a converted storefront and boarding house, hence the eight bedrooms upstairs. I think now about those windows and realize that we could have easily been sliced in two if one of them was ever broken. The entire house was heated with a wood stove attached to the cooking stove in the kitchen. In time, a gas space heater was added in the living room. The single bathroom was upstairs and at the opposite end of the house, so it received little heat and, in the winter, offered a frosty experience. I lived in that house until I met and married my first husband. I often dream I am in that house, and in spite of the Spartan and Stoic ethic that prevailed, I love those dreams because I loved that house.

I do remember quite vividly my grandmother taught me to do embroidery. In time, I also learned to crochet, but that skill was taught to me by a neighbor. One other passion my grandmother and I shared was the big garden in the side yard. I do not remember working with her, but I do remember hours spent weeding and picking flowers, and I loved the solitude. To this day, my garden work is my mental health regimen. My brother Jim was born six years after we moved in, and my grandmother died three years after that. Before she died, she told me to take care of the garden when she was gone, and I did.

Over the years, as I have matured, my view of Grandmother Mary has softened. Do not get me wrong; she was tough as nails, but I came to see that her pragmatism was how she survived. I did not understand all the circumstances of her life until many years later, in part, because no one talked about her marriage and life with Adam. In addition, it is only as I progressed through life and confronted the realities of a less than ideal marriage and raising children alone that I was awed at what she accomplished in the 1920s and '30s. In addition, my Amanda Irene is my mother, and so I came to realize the challenges that confronted Grandma Mary in raising, shall I say, a difficult child.

The woman I met had been through a great deal of difficulty, shame, and sorrow (she buried four children) much like Grandma Emma. I believe she simply had developed a survival instinct. Just like I do not remember her saying "I love you" neither did I hear her lament her fate, adopt a victim mentality, and/or wallow in self-pity. Finally, she passed on the Roman Catholic faith to me, through my mother, and that has saved my life on many occasions. I have a lovely photograph of her as an eighteen-year-old, and I see a physical resemblance between us. She was young and hopeful in that picture because it was taken before her marriage to Adam.

To begin with, my maternal grandfather Adam is difficult to trace because he immigrated to the United States. He was born in 1875–76 to John and Angela (Clocek), and their birth places are listed as Russia-Poland. On August 24, 1908, he married my grandmother Mary. These are the only "facts" I possess about him, and they were taken from a copy of their marriage license that I obtained two years ago. Until I received this document, I had no idea what his parents' names were. I was also interested to see that Grandmother Mary's parents, Frank and Francis, were also from Russia-Poland. (Her parents were another part of Grandma Mary's story because her mother died when she was very young, and she supposedly had a wicked stepmother.) As the story unfolds, this interest will become clearer.

Growing up, my mother told me she was her father's favorite, but her memories of him were limited because he died when she was nine years old. I heard stories, predominately from my Uncle Harry, about how Adam was not allowed in the military in World War I because if he was captured, the Russians might not let him come back to the US. Uncle Harry told the wondrous tale I recounted earlier about the Cossack soldiers and collecting severed heads in a sack. You must admit my family was colorful, if nothing else, with shades of *Dr. Zhivago*.

There was a very illuminating tale about Adam told to me by my mother while I was in high school. This story did not come voluntarily from the dear woman. She was so provoked by another woman's memory of Adam as "…the life of the party and beloved of the ladies…" She spewed her story to me like Vesuvius erupting before she could stop herself. It was a scandal that, according to my mother, cost Adam his properties, carpentry business, and, worst of all, his reputation. I do believe this was also the unnamed reason that Uncle Harry changed his last name.

The story was that there were three male friends, A, B, and C, one of which was Adam who we shall call Friend A. Friend B had a wife, and apparently, Friend C found her quite attractive, and they began a liaison. Well, B became suspicious and confronted his wife. The wife wanted to protect C, so she told B that she was involved with A. B confronted A in a bar/tavern. By my mother's account, he was as innocent as the driven snow. A denied the charge and called the wife of B a whore and other unsavory names for all the tavern patrons to hear.

This public display led to a libel case, and Adam, who built houses in Dunkirk, lost it all but the home in which his family lived. (The house I moved into was not that house; my grandmother sold that place, *but* I lived in it later with husband 2.) No one employed Adam either, so Mary was left to work seven days a week, with two Sundays off a month, as a cook and cleaner for the Sisters of Saint Joseph. Adam began to fill his days with alcohol, and he died in 1931. Did I tell you how much I hate alcohol? I think I did, but it bears repeating here.

I was told this story once and only once, but I understood and remembered every word. My mother swore me to secretary, and she never spoke of it to me again. I have held my peace all these many years until now. So instead of telling someone, I am writing it in a book. Good thing Mom is not around because she would probably not be so happy. If I am telling secrets, I might as well add a new thing I learned about my mother when I got her birth certificate. Her given name is Irena (quite Russian sounding, eh?), not Irene. Not a big deal but interesting just the same.

In this vein, I do need to add something that happened just the other day. For the eight years since my mother died, I have had Adam and Mary's wedding picture hanging on the wall in my family room. I had company over recently who asked about the picture, and I was pointing out the individuals. I took it down yesterday and looked at it yet again, and lo and behold, I noticed three things I had missed all these years. One was the elegance of the wedding attire. It was very formal, elaborate, and, dare I say, rich-looking. Grandmother Mary's dress was beautiful and full of lace, an expensive commodity in 1908. Next, the best man and matron of honor were a married couple; it was written on the back of the picture and on the marriage license. I thought my great aunt Ann, Mary's sister, was the maid of honor. Who was this couple? Could it be B and his wife?

The last thing I noticed was very subtle. The picture was taken in August of 1908, and Grandma must have been dying with the heat in that dress because it covered her head to toe, and there was no air conditioning. Everyone was very straight-faced, formally attired, and stood ramrod straight, everyone except Adam. He had a casual stance, shoulders slouched to his left side, slight smile (dare it; call it a smirk), and his left hand in his side pocket. He was handsome, the best looking of the three men in the picture, and his body language told me he knew it! How had I missed that? I just know when he walked, he had a swagger—the mysterious Russian Pole who escaped from the Cassocks and severed heads. How hard he fell when he was sued and lost his life's work and reputation. I do wonder just how faithful he was to Mary. Humility did not seem to be a virtue he embraced easily, so I believe he self-medicated with alcohol until life could not hurt him anymore.

The Russian-Polish heritage, hence "Lara's Theme" was another mystery, and I got a partial answer from PBS. About two years ago, PBS broadcast a series entitled *The Story of the Jews with Simon Schama.* That documentary spent a good amount of time showing the ever-changing national boundaries of Poland and Russia in the nineteenth century. Adam's confused heritage between Polish and Russian, as well as Grandma Mary's parents, made a great deal more sense. In addition, the fact that this special was on the history of the

Jewish race was not lost on me. I wondered if Adam was fluent in both Russian and Polish. The political turmoil of the area during the nineteenth century, including pogroms against the Jewish people, gave further fuel to my wondering about a Jewish heritage, hidden by a baptism, from his side of the family.

I have another factor I want to add. I know this is not anything but antidotal evidence, but over the years, I have questioned my deep emotional reaction to the story and the music of *Fiddler on the Roof* (1964). If you remember my reaction to the military band made up of injured soldiers, then you understand the depth of emotion I felt. I have been in love with the musical *Fiddler on the Roof* since it premiered on Broadway. I bought the original cast recording/record with Zero Mostel and drove my mother crazy with it because I played it until I knew every word to every song. My daughters and I used to dance through the house singing *Matchmaker*, and they grew up loving it. In fact, Amanda just mentioned that she sings entire songs from *Fiddler on the Roof* to a Jewish colleague when he is having a bad day. I have seen it on stage twice, both times with Amanda, but not on Broadway. This year, *Fiddler* is back on Broadway, and I was given a ticket to see it as a birthday gift. Mazel tof!

In addition, my DNA test came back. Now the results were reported based on five geographic areas: Europe, Central/South America, the Middle East/North Africa, Africa, and Asia. I have listed the areas in the order they were reported to me with Europe being my strongest DNA link and Asia the least. Just based on what you read in this memoir, you are thinking, Well, yes of course. Each of the countries included in the groupings are then listed in order with the strongest DNA match for my DNA listed first. Europe was no surprise, but the country was, wait for it...Belgium. Scotland (9), Ireland (6), Poland (19), and Russia (24) were not in the top five of the twenty-five countries listed.

The site has a disclaimer about ancestry. They use an algorithm to match me to folks in areas with DNA markers most like mine. I am including this explanation because for the Middle East/North Africa group, which was the third areas in strength, I had Israel as the first country listed. *Okay*, so if this is not about ancestry, at least, it seems that my DNA matches most closely in the Middle East/North Africa folks in Israel. I can tell you this information would make my mother go crazy and not for happiness.

I also have an antidotal story to lend credence to this conclusion. Shortly after getting these DNA results, I had my annual physical. My physician is Jewish, the Jewish New Year (Rosh Hashanah) was near, so I wished him *L'shanah Tovah* (Happy New Year). He looked at me and said, "Are you religious?" I hesitated and said, "No" and then added, "I am a good Catholic girl." I then told him about my DNA result and my ticket to see *Fiddler on the Roof*. He said, "You look like you belong to the tribe." I was beaming from ear-to-ear. When I was leaving, after receiving a clean bill of health, I shook his hand and wished him happy holidays. He told me, "You are one of us, so enjoy your holidays too." That was the best doctor visit ever.

Is this positive proof? No, it is not. When I put it all together, it is still rather circumstantial but somewhat compelling. I just simply do not believe in coincidences, and when I remain true to that trait, I seem to do my best detective work. Why did I suddenly look at that wedding picture again and read the body language of Adam? I have examined that picture many times before. I love watching detective shows, and from them, I have learned not to overlook the slightest clue. The most insightful information may well be right under our noses if we only ask why and go beyond just looking and really see what is in front of us. Remember Pappy and his dead boss? I would have never discovered this if I had not been curious about the employer listed on his social security application.

So what have I discovered thus far? There seems to be corpses related to my two grandfathers. Pappy's pictures, or what I have identified as him, seem to have that same, "I am the smartest man in the room" look that Adam had. Their lives are full of unanswered questions, and the more I discover about them, the less I realize that I know. Perhaps more information will be revealed before I complete this memoir. Stay tuned!

I will close this chapter with a memory of Adam's funeral recounted by my mother. She was nine years old, and she remembered being in church, ready to follow his coffin down the aisle, and she was crying. Her older brother Benny (Bernard) looked at her and said, "Don't waste your tears on that son of a b———." Benny's remark, in church no less, was probably a result of an earlier incident when Adam attempted to stab him and his brother Roger with a butcher knife. He was holding the knife behind his back, and as the incident was recounted to me, Grandmother Mary calmly walked up to him, put out her hand, and said, "Adam, give it to me," and he did. I tell you the woman was tough as nails just like Dr. Zhivago's Lara.

Chapter 18

IS THAT ALL THERE IS?

Is that all there is?
Is that all there is?
If that's all there is my friends
Then let's keep dancing
Let's break out the booze and have a ball
If that's all there is.
(Jerry Leiber and Mike Stoller [1969], Is That All
   There Is?)

This song was first made famous by Peggy Lee when it was released as the title song of an album of the same name. I was always fascinated by the absolute desolation of spirit and nihilism the lyrics represent. In my mind, the person singing these lyrics could easily be screaming, "Hey, you get off my cloud" at the same time. How often have we heard, "Eat, drink, and be merry for tomorrow we may die?" This is a variation on the same theme—a kind of continuum of hopelessness. On one end, we have the manic eat, drink, and be merry crowd and on the other end, the depressed and the "Is that all there is?" crowd. So you are asking why am I taking on such a moribund topic?

I have alluded to similar sentiments as I presented the stories for my ancestors. Grandma Emma seemed to be totally overwhelmed by her life, and I can only suspect, based on the clues she left me, her state of mind at the end of her life. I envision her as an "Is that all there is?" person. On the other hand, Pappy too saw his share of loss. His mother died when he was fourteen months old; he married late in life and buried his stillborn son John. I can only guess at the course of his life because he left far fewer clues for me than Emma, but I believe he seemed to be at the manic end of the spectrum.

Then you consider that both people were the parents of my father Frank with Emma dying when he was seven years old. Then when my parents marry, you add my grandfather, Adam, to the mix, yikes! According to the current psychological theory, I should be poor or homeless or drug and/or alcohol addicted, or all of the above because of the loss and dysfunction that preceded me. I personally do not accept this prognosis, and I know that before Great-Granddad George, the Paige family, at least, was not only functional but also prominent as well.

I know the nature versus nurture argument will go on long after my two fingers have typed the last word of this memoir. I guess it is all a matter of perspective and not letting yourself be defined by other human beings. Please do not get me wrong. The fastest way to "Is that all there is?" land is by cutting yourself off from other people—aka "Hey you get off my cloud!" If you know who you are and have identified the gift only you bear for the world, then you can interact without being controlled by others. Oh, sometimes, we are fooled by manipulators, but the secret is to *learn* from those encounters; some controlling people are very subtle indeed. I must admit that, over the years, I have learned a great deal about this subject. In my early life, I was often disgusted with myself for being taken in yet again. For a time, I saw myself as a hopeless mess—yes, even a victim. As you can see, I did not give into this mindset and learned enough to write this memoir.

My point is I am none of these things. I have had my fair share of difficulties, and upon reflection, many were self-inflicted. However, despite the massive amounts of alcohol consumed by my ancestors, I have never been drunk. Of course, there is the polio, family drama with my parents, and my own marriage miscues. However, during all of this apparent chaos, I have endured to complete my education; I hold down a somewhat prestigious position as a college professor, and now I am writing this book to reflect about it. I have embraced the adjective resilient—some have called it stubborn—as a personal characteristic; I guess it makes me wonder where resilience comes from. In other words, why do some people's lives sing, "Is that all there is?" and others are singing "Amazing Grace?"

I know you are thinking, *Here, she goes again.* I do think grace is part of the answer. I read a fascinating research study the other day about women, depression, and suicide. It seems that the women in the study (during 1996 to 2010) who attend church at least once a week were five times less likely to commit suicide, and the women who did not have regular church attendance were seven times more likely to die younger than Catholic women. Catholic women who attend church at least twice a week had *zero* suicides during that period. By the way, just identifying as a Catholic, without attending church, had no effect on the rate of suicide (*LA Times* June 29, 2016). You will forgive me if I bask in the Catholic glow here. This is not bad for a medieval, ineffective, male-dominated, and has-been religion.

I find this fascinating because I know academics, and this is not the result they were expecting. So for these research results to be published in a peer-reviewed journal and then in the *LA Times* clearly indicates to me the power of the data. I had begun to suspect something along these lines years ago. I pondered the victim equals depression/suicide meme that pervaded the mental health profession. If this outcome was so inevitable, then why were there no mass (pardon the pun) suicides after the concentration camps were liberated after World War II? I know there were psychological effects from this horrific experience, but it did not lead everyone, if not most of the survivors, to commit suicide. In the same vein, I have heard that those who have religious faith have a better rate of physical recovery from sickness and injuries. These findings about faith explode the entire victim mentality. I believe that instead of a lifetime of counseling and consuming pharmaceuticals, going to Mass more than once a week might be a cheaper and more effective option.

I also have a tale of two states as well. As you know, I am awaiting Great-Granddad George's death certificate for GSMD from the state of Rhode Island. In addition, I thought I might as well request Emma's birth certificate from Pennsylvania while I was at it. Both initial requests were returned to me because I sent them to the wrong office. I sent them out a second time and waited.

The first request to come back to me was from Pennsylvania. The office I was referred to only has records back to 1893, and Emma was born in 1889. Without going into all the emails, I still did not find out who had the records before 1893; it is like a historical black hole. You have read enough to know I have been at this genealogy searching for a while, so I am no neophyte at this stuff, and I was baffled with this dead end. Neither the DAR nor the GSMD have requested Emma's birth certificate, but now, the search has become a challenge. Then I discovered the state of Pennsylvania did not require birth records prior to 1893. They say truth is stranger than fiction, and I cannot imagine what a mess searches like mine would be if this was the practice throughout eighteenth and nineteenth America. However, this information would explain how, when Emma was married to Charles, years were eliminated from her age so she was closer in age to Charles.

Now I ask you to contrast this to my Rhode Island encounter. I was sure I would have a parallel experience, and I was very pleasantly surprised. There in my mailbox was an envelope, and it was thin. I have learned thick envelopes mean they are returning all my data and telling me to go elsewhere. The cover sheet was a checklist informing me that the state does two initial genealogical searches for the price of the copy—$2! They advised me that I was to send them the $2 because they returned my $20 check. The second sheet was a copy of the death certificate with a shiny gold seal. Can you imagine they trusted me for the $2?

The check immediately went out in the mail with a *big* thank you for trusting me to send the money. It was such a bargain that I wished I had one more relative in Rhode Island to take advantage of the price; it was like a genealogical sale. The one surprise on the certificate was Great-Granddad's cause of death: senility. I always thought dying had a physical source. Many people have dementia and are otherwise in good physical health. Now I could imagine a person wandering away, injuring themselves, and dying from their injuries not from the senility. Oh well, I guess it is just another oddity in the Paige family genealogy. At any rate, I was able to send the scanned certificate to GSMD; it was the last piece of documentation they requested, and I am relieved this is done. So now I wait.

Now I ask you what did I take from this experience? During this process of tracking down documents, I could go to the "woe is me" mindset, or I can count my blessings. I did have some "moments" that are well-documented in this memoir like when I was confused about Granddad George. However, I can almost guarantee you, from personal experience, that the victim mentality is a self-fulfilling prophesy. Even the most blessed of lives will have setbacks. Resilient folks just take it in stride and move on with their lives. I do not think things are "just easier for some people." The reality is they just complain less than the victim. In time, these folks might even discover that this setback worked to their advantage (Romans 8:28). The victim sees these occurrences as a "see, I told you so" moment. From my perspective, they miss their opportunities because they are waiting for the next shoe to fall, and do not get me started on the curse of fear.

This reality about life's ups and downs reminds me of a story told about the Catholic mystic St. Teresa of Avila. The story goes that she was said to be having difficulty during a trip. She said to God, "Oh, God, when will You cease from scattering obstacles in our path?" She heard God say, "Do not complain, daughter, this is how I treat my friends." Her response was, "It is on that account that You have so few" (https://fauxtations.wordpress.com/2016/10/03/st-teresa-of-avila-if-this-is-how-you-treat-your-friends/). Why add this tale? Just to assure you that God's grace does not eliminate obstacles but rather includes difficulty. Remember it was Jesus who sent the apostles out on the Sea of Galilee only to have them caught in a bad storm and fearing for their lives (Matthew 14:22–33).

I would like to discover Grandma Emma's birth record, but I need to cool down and let the whole thing rest for a while. I have many other things to keep me busy, so I do know, in fact, that is not all that there is for me. Keeping all your eggs in one basket is not a good idea anyway. Often, when I just let my mind focus elsewhere, a new possibility will emerge from a place in which, initially, I only saw chaos.

    I wish I could attest to the reality that I never sink into the "Is that all there is?" mindset. The difference today is I do not pitch a tent and take up residence there. I love the term John Bunyan used in his book *Pilgrim's Progress* (Get it? Pilgrim and *Mayflower?*) to describe this place—The Slough of Despond—aka the swamp of despair. I need to keep reminding myself that I cannot change the past, but I can use my mistakes to inform my future choices. It sounds so easy, right? My life philosophy boils down to the bromide that life is simple, but it is not easy. Think about that one for a while, and I will continue to wait for the next chapter in my story to evolve.

Chapter 19

ANTICIPATION: PART 2

> And tomorrow we might not be together
> I'm no prophet and I don't know nature's ways
> So I'll try and see into your eyes right now
> And stay right here 'cause these are the good old
>   days (These are the good old days)
> And stay right here 'cause these are the good old
>   days
> (These are the good old days)
> (These are the good old days)
> (These are the good old days)
> (These are…the good old days)
> (Carly Simon [1971], Anticipation)

If you have been paying attention, you are thinking, *She used this tune already*! In response, I will applaud your attention to detail. In my defense, I will suggest that works of art, especially music, use a melodic theme that is woven throughout the piece/movements. Music is the metaphor that I employ throughout this memoir, so it is entirely consistent to reuse one of my tunes. If you pay attention, you will also note that I used different lyrics. Chapter 13 takes the lyrics from the beginning of the song, and this chapter from the end of the song.

Can you guess why I reused this lyric? If you read what I have written up to this point, I am pretty sure you know exactly why I picked this lyric. Admittedly, when the melody drifts through my mind, the first thought I have is of the ketchup commercial from the 1970s. It is a tribute to the marketing folks that, so many years later, this ad is firmly fastened in my long-term memory. Their point was that their product, so thick and tasty, was worth the wait as it came out of the bottle. I need to fold that thought into my impatient mind as I await word on my applications to the DAR and the GSMD. We are approaching two months, and in my world, that is literally an eternity.

I have been busy during these summer months, so that has helped me pass the time. The first event was my two day fiftieth high school class reunion in Dunkirk. Way back in chapter 1, I wrote about my tending of graves in Dunkirk. Since I have written those words, I have selected cemetery plots in Dunkirk, in the cemetery of my mother's parish, for my brother, my son, and I. (The three of us reject cremation, and the plots are in the same cemetery where my parents are buried.) While in Dunkirk for the reunion, I attended Mass at my mother's parish church.

This was the first time I was in this church since my mother's funeral eight years ago, and I lost it. I was not hysterical or disruptive during Mass. Halfway through the Mass, my tears began to flow unabated. Everywhere I looked in the church, there was a memory: my father's funeral, my brother's wedding, my return to the Catholic Church after a seven-year absence, my two youngest children's baptism, my mother's funeral, and countless holiday (Christmas and Easter) Masses since 1981. If nothing else, this event reassured me that I had made the right choice about the cemetery plots, and my reunion reminded me that Dunkirk was still my home.

Earlier, I wrote about my abrupt arrival in Dunkirk when I was four years old—seeing snow for the first time and moving in with the strangers who were my mother's family. All my K-12 school years were spent in Dunkirk, and the folks at my reunion went back to those days. My elementary years were completed in a small Catholic school, but high school was spent with these people. There were a few individuals who crossed over both my school experiences however. It was amazing to me that at the reunion (a) we did not look as bad as I anticipated, (b) we remembered/recognized one another (both because we still looked somewhat the same and we just plain remembered), and (c) within mere moments of meeting, we were back fifty years and acting like was saw each other every day.

I spent a great deal of the two days, including Mass, with a close friend from high school. She revealed that we were in first grade together, and she remembered my leg brace. I was surprised because (a) I was just being made aware that our friendship went further than I realized, and yet I still do not remember her from those days. (b) She shared the memory of my leg brace from my polio with me, and (c) her husband was a polio survivor. There is something about finding out that someone else shares a deep and personal memory. Remember Grandma Emma instructed me to "bring the family together." It was suddenly crystal clear to me that sharing memories about one another is a far more profound and an easy way to bring people together. When I began this book, I thought that bringing the family together literally required me to move graves around! I realize that I was gradually moving toward this realization during this family genealogy search, but it was deeply reinforced from this unexpected source.

The second reunion event that relates to this memoir came from another high school friend who was attending our reunion for the first time. It was my understanding she was somewhat reluctant to attend, but I know by the end that she left feeling quite different. She and I were having breakfast on the first morning, and we were catching up with each other's lives. Eventually, she revealed that she was a member of the DAR! The discovery was like setting a match to dry tinder, and I was telling her about my genealogical findings. She belongs to the Lexington, Massachusetts (as in *the shot heard around the world*) DAR affiliate, and she loves being part of the organization. This revelation just reignited my own fire, and we parted with promises to keep in touch over this shared love. Again, I found a common experience with another individual that reinforced my own discoveries about genealogy.

The third event occurred when I took a trip to New Mexico to visit my "baby" brother Jim and his wife Linda. I flew from New York to Albuquerque, and as we made the final descent, we flew through a big fluffy cloud. I am not sure if I can explain the feeling that overcame me, but it involved the (Paige) Cloud. I was in a real cloud, and though I did not see or hear anyone, I felt a profound connection to the ancestors. I am afraid this is as far as words will take me, but I know that I will carry this memory with me for the rest of my days. Tears filled my eyes, and somehow the ethereal environment of the cloud took me a step away from the landlocked life that we spend on earth and a small step closer to the heavenly realm.

In addition, when I was mentally recalling this experience, I was reminded of yet another scripture reference that I overlooked in a prior chapter: "Therefore, since we are surrounded by so great a crowd of witnesses let us rid ourselves of every burden and sin that clings to us and persevere in running the race that lies before us" (Hebrews 12:1 NAB). This scripture ties together all the experiences of this chapter, and I wish I could take some credit for this, but I simply cannot. Like so much of this memoir, I simply began to write and followed where my two fingers took me.

The most obvious connection is the reference to a cloud. The metaphor fits on so many levels it is beginning to feel less like a metaphor and more like a literal truth. As that airplane descended, I felt a brush with or a proximity to those witnesses. I should add that at the moment of this experience, I had my nose firmly planted in a novel, and my thoughts were far away from the (Paige) Cloud. I had a window seat, and as I felt the descent, I simply looked up to see what was happening, and I was literally surrounded by a cloud and, dare I say, witnesses. Remember my story in a prior chapter about my making hash brown potatoes and feeling Pappy's presence? The same type of experience occurred this time but heightened by several degrees of magnitude.

The other theme Hebrews 12:1 refers to is perseverance and/or resilience. Based on my own experiences, my advice to you is when you are knocked down, you are not knocked out. When life knocks you down, the secret is to get up, dust yourself off, check your bearings, and keep going. I questioned my decision to pursue a PhD so many times during those seven years. I still marvel that I ever finished it, but I did. Was the dissertation my best work? No, it was not even close, but it was good enough to earn a PhD and to have my dissertation published in a peer-reviewed journal. There were so many times that I felt so alone during those years, but now I know I was not. I had an interested "peanut gallery" (for those of you who remember that term from the *Howdy Doody Show*), and I know they were on my side all the way.

Another aspect of my family task occurred to me when, shortly after my return from New Mexico, I spent a week at my son and daughter-in-law's home. Brayden (age ten) and Cade (age four) were in need of childcare, and I said yes to their request for assistance. I will admit I had some trepidations about my limited mobility with two active boys, but an in-ground swimming pool (the week was beastly hot) was the perfect solution. Suddenly, I began to realize this week was another opportunity to "bring the family together."

I needed to expand my view of this task because, up to this point, I had been looking to people who came before me. I was so frustrated by how little I knew about the Paige family (Who raised Pappy? How did Pappy meet Emma? How did Pappy get to Philadelphia?), and I realized all these questions emerged because no one recounted the stories and/or had memories of these events. I realized that I needed to apply this concept to the here and now in my own life. I no longer had the capacity to impact yesterday. I had today to make a difference, and I had to make the most of my opportunities.

If I became too preoccupied with the past, I would miss opportunities in the present to create connections and memories with my own family members and friends. In all the events I recounted in this chapter (the reunion, my brother Jim in New Mexico, and the week with my grandsons), I spent a great deal of time (a) remembering past events, (b) sharing current events to catch up, and (c) projecting the future. I know my grandsons got to know me better, and I got to know them. I spent time with them, as never before, without their parents around, and that was very important because it involved developing a personal relationship that only they and I shared. If that is not bringing the family together, then I do not know what is.

My last thought for this chapter is this lull in my quest, and my heightened level of anticipation was really a good thing. Hindsight, as they say, is always twenty-twenty. Like the ketchup ad, my rich and thick experiences are worth the wait. During this wait, more was revealed to me about the reality of this earthly life and the connection to the next life.

There was a motion picture recently titled *Heaven Is for Real* (2014). It is based on a true story of a four-year-old boy who died on the operating table and experienced and connected with family members he neither knew in this life (his father's granddad) nor ever knew of their existence (a sister that was miscarried before he was born) but met in Heaven. I believe this movie represents the eternity we will have to share memories and fill in the blanks (see my questions above). I need to share the information I have learned about the past with my contemporaries and share my own story with those I love and trust.

If I die with all this information in my head, the family will not be any closer to coming together. So now I begin to see my task from my grandmother Emma as two-pronged. First, I must share my genealogical discoveries so the stories of those who came before us remain alive. Second, I must share my own story.

Look at how overwhelmed I was when I was confronted by the memories in my mother's parish church. I am sure this was enhanced by all the memories that were refreshed by my class reunion and writing this memoir. All these experiences caused me to reflect recently on the notion that to be forgotten, after our death, is a horrible fate. If our lives make the world a better place, then our memory will linger in the hearts and minds of others. This knowledge is the foundation of the hope that has the potential to take me through my difficulties. However, if I choose to set up camp in the Slough of Despond, contemplate my belly button, and scream, "Hey, you get off of my cloud!" then I am indeed lost.

Chapter 20

WE ARE THE CHAMPIONS

> But it's been no bed of roses
> No pleasure cruise
> I consider it a challenge before the whole human
>   race
> And I ain't gonna lose
> We are the champions, my friends
> And we'll…
> We are the champions, my friends
> And we'll keep on fighting 'til the end
> We are the champions
> We are the champions
> No time for losers
> 'Cause we are the champions of the world
> (Freddy Mercury [1977], *News of the World*)

Unless you have spent most of your life in hibernation and/or isolation, this lyric and melody from the British rock band Queen should be quite familiar. For many years, this lyric has been used at the end of tournament events as the anthem to celebrate the victory of their new champion. In addition, I have used it in my classes as an example of a power anthem because the victor(s) is (are) portrayed as spent. He/she/they are physically, mentally, and emotionally drained from the competitive ordeal. Queen portrays victory as a hard-fought battle that is as much about persistence as it is about ability or cunning, and I believe it can be an anthem about a person like me. I am not the smartest person, but I am probably one of the most stubborn persons you will ever meet. Stubborn, when focused on a good and noble cause, is a blessing, but when it is focused on an unworthy end, stubbornness leads to disaster. I did not read about this in a book and have recounted some of my personal experience with the latter in this memoir.

It has been nearly a month since I wrote my last chapter. In the interim, I made daily anxious trips to my mailbox only to find no correspondence from the DAR and the GSMD. I was frustrated, to say the least. In addition, the "What ifs…" began to creep into my thinking. I know where the weak links are in my genealogy records: Pappy and my dad. I hoped Pappy's birth certificate, with no name, and the missing marriage license for Pappy and Emma were not going to undo my application. Worse, if they made my membership contingent on producing either document, I had no idea how to proceed. My mother putting the wrong name for her mother-in-law on Dad's death certificate did not contribute to my peace of mind either.

I had lots of time to tear the whole search apart and reduce it to meaningless gibberish. I did finally send an email to both groups. GSMD responded that it would be, at minimum, another month. I received nothing from DAR making my paranoia even worse. Two weeks later, I sent another email to the registrar Donna because I knew the summer hiatus for DAR was over, and I needed to find the time and date for the next meeting. The first line of her response was, "Congratulations, you are now a member."

I had to sit and stare at the computer screen and let this news sink in because it took time to wash away all the "What ifs…?" I had collected. Next came my smile and finally the tears. I had grown afraid to embrace the colonel as my ancestor because if I were unable to create a link through the DAR, then it would always be in question. Maybe it is foolish of me, but the approval of my lineage by the DAR was an important validation, beyond my own opinion, that my claims to Colonel Timothy Paige were legitimate. In addition, I was already a patriot, and so I did not take unsubstantiated claims lightly.

I have always loved history, but in the last year, the Revolutionary War period has captivated me. Did the colonel know George Washington? Alexander Hamilton? Thomas Jefferson? Benjamin Franklin? Did they know the colonel? Did they respect the colonel? What did the colonel contribute to the revolutionary cause? In addition to his military service, the colonel was a member of the Committee of Correspondence in the Massachusetts area, so he was more than a participant in the Revolutionary War; he was a leader. The other thing I reflect on was that most of the colonists were not actively committed to the separation of the American colonies from England. In such a tight group, it is hard to imagine the colonel not having contact with the other leaders and that there are far fewer of their descendants than one might think.

As I am writing this memoir, *Hamilton* is the hottest ticket on Broadway. Again, if you are still hibernating and/or isolated, then you would not know what I am writing about. As the title suggests, the musical show is based on the life and death of Alexander Hamilton. I have a ticket to see it on Broadway in a few months. (If you are still wondering what I am referring to because you have never heard of Alexander Hamilton, check out *Wikipedia*.) I have never been to a Broadway theater in New York City, so this is the first check mark on my bucket list. The same weekend, we are also seeing *Fiddler on the Roof*; remember my affinity to all things Jewish? This is like a Family Heritage Festival weekend for me. Even better, I am seeing it with my friend Jane who I have referred to several times in this memoir.

I have always loved live theater; thanks in part to my parents who introduced me to it when I was in my early teens. I also think I am safe in speculating that my mother learned to love the theater from Dad—remember their first date was the opera—because none of her family members have a particular interest in live theater. My point is that my desire to see *Hamilton* is not due solely to my DAR membership, but it was certainly enhanced by it. Alexander Hamilton died because of a gunshot wound sustained in a duel with Aaron Burr. The play is somewhat sympathetic to Burr, the former

US vice president, and the man who shot Hamilton. Burr's reality was he was tried and acquitted for treason and died in disgrace. All this knowledge has been resurrected from high school American history, and the catalyst was the DAR. I honestly cannot get enough of it.

I had another point to ponder as well. The lyrics of Queen's anthem refer to "*We* are the champions." At first, that bothered me because I was not sure it was the best word choice for this chapter. I guess my search had some teamwork involved, like the help I received from Jane, but for the most part, it has been a long, lonely slog. I could change the lyric to "I am the champion..." but that just was not right either. Then it occurred to me that the lyric is exactly perfect because the "we" is me and the folks in the (Paige) Cloud.

I may be getting closer than ever to Grandma Emma's directive of bringing the family together. Look at the things that I know about now, and I am even writing this memoir about it to tell others. I now see myself as part of them, and they are part of me. I have felt their closeness at various times during the search.

1. Pappy visits me when I make home fries.
2. I found myself visualizing Pappy's funeral at Mount Moriah Cemetery in March of 1947.
3. I felt them all as I was descending through the *clouds* on my airline trip to New Mexico.
4. I experienced the tragedy that seemed to be a constant companion of Grandma Emma as she moved from youthful optimism to middle age despair.
5. I came to know of Emma's firstborn Aunt Edna/Ruth and how much she was like my father.
6. I discovered that when Emma's parents died, she was never mentioned in their obituaries like they wanted to forget she existed. All I say is not anymore.
7. George Paige and Louisa Blanchard's family were broken up when Louisa died.

The family of my Great Uncle George Paige now know he had a long-lost brother Frank, aka Pappy, and he had a family, and here we are! Because of the DAR, the connection to the rest of the Paige family was established. Correct me if I am wrong, but this sure sounds like bringing the family together.

Chapter 21

OH, THE BLOOMING BLOODY SPIDER

> Oh, the blooming, bloody spider went up the spider web,
> The blooming, bloody rain came down and washed the spider out,
> The blooming, bloody sun came out and dried up all the rain,
> And the blooming, bloody spider came up the web again.

This may not be the version of this children's song as you know it, but now, it captures my mood perfectly, and it is so English. According to Wikipedia, this is the original lyric found in *Camp and camino in Lower California* (1910). Just like the blooming bloody spider, I thought I was approaching the end of the sticky web I refer to as a memoir. Two weeks ago, I ended the previous chapter awaiting final word on my DAR membership, and I was ever so hopeful that my GSMD would follow shortly. I should reassure you that nothing has arisen to dash those hopes. So what, you might ask, had gotten me so riled up?

Some of you may have had the experience that when you have spent a great deal of time on a project, it is difficult not to want to continue the experience. As I have written, oh, so many times, waiting is not my strong suit, so I began to wonder if I could put my newfound genealogical skills to further use. Of course, this whole experience began with my nocturnal visit from Grandma Emma, so I thought I could tie up some ends with her family and maybe make some of the same kind of connections I made with the Paige side. But before I can tell you why I am feeling like a blooming bloody spider caught in her own web, I must recount an experience that may or may not have relevance to this story.

When I was gathering the documentation for the DAR and the GSMD, both groups made it very clear that they wanted birth, death, and marriage certificates back three generations. So my task was to spend dollars and get these documents for Dad and Mom, Pappy and Emma, and Great-Granddad George and Louisa. I have recounted my various ordeals in obtaining these records in prior chapters, so I will not write it all again. I submitted what I had, and to date, the DAR accepted my documentation. Emma's information was bothering me however. She is in the Paige line because she married Pappy. Feeling restless, I decided to try to obtain her birth certificate. I began by writing to the state of Pennsylvania with an application and a check requesting Emma's birth certificate. The state sent both back and told me I had to apply to the county. The county directed me to the Register of Wills. I received a letter from them informing me they only had birth records from 1893–1906 (Emma was born in 1889). However, the same letter informed me about the process for obtaining birth records. This ambiguity bothered me, so using the email address in the letter, I wrote for clarification and to see if I needed to waste another first-class stamp.

This is where the story gets strange. You have read enough of this memoir to know that I can be stubborn, so instead of abandoning the search, I proceeded with renewed vigor. I do not consider myself an expert in these matters, but I was getting pretty darn good. The email I sent to the Register of Wills kept bouncing back to me as undeliverable, so after about five tries, I called the office. The person I needed to talk to was out, so I left a message requesting clarification. After a week, there was no response to the phone call, but I finally got an email through. I will not reproduce the series of emails that followed, but suffice it to say, there was a very strange tone to them. They were somewhat condescending and implied that if I was smart enough, I would not be making these inquiries. There were other sources recommended for birth documentation; I followed them, and they were all dead ends. It just seemed incredible to me that persons born in this county before 1893 had no birth records.

The point that I want to get to here is the person I was corresponding with had the same last name as the maiden name of Emma's sister-in-law (married to her brother John). I made a comment in one of my emails about this possible connection between the writer and myself, but there was no response to my comment, just the implied, "Are you done yet?" I know this is flimsy coincidence, but hold this thought while I tell you how I got to be the blooming bloody spider (and remember, spiders spin webs).

This past week, I pulled out Emma's file and thought I would look for family connections because her birth record seemed to be such a fruitless effort. I began by trying to find Emma's siblings, so I checked my great grandparents' obituaries; remember, there was no mention of Emma in either of them. So Emma had a brother born in 1891, a sister born in 1893, and another brother born in 1908. There was quite a span between the sister and youngest brother, but that was not unusual, so I thought nothing about it. Remember the limitation on birth records (1893–1906) for this county, and I had no desire to renew my acquaintance with the county bureaucrat, so I was not about to follow up on the older brother and sister.

In the databases, I was finding nothing much on the older brother and sister, and then I found the birth certificate for the youngest brother. The date was right, so I expected to see the names of my great grandparents listed as his parents, but they were not. His mother was Emma. The father had a different name, so they were not married, and the child was given Emma's surname. (A little more searching for information on the father and I found out he worked for the railroad just like my great-grandfather.) Remember, in the obituaries, this youngest brother was listed as their son while Emma is never mentioned. But there is more. The last name of the doctor who delivered him is the same last name as Emma's sister-in-law, and the reluctant bureaucrat *and* the clerk who signed the birth certificate has the same last name as the maiden name of the sister-in-law's mother. Give yourself a minute to let all this sink in; believe me, it took me some time, but in a small rural county, all bets are off. In addition, remember, I am only paranoid when I am wrong.

Now, maybe, this revelation will not have the same effect on you as it had on me, but at that moment, I became the blooming bloody spider. I thought I had negotiated all the twist and turns of this spider web, and boom, a whole new revelation—down came the rain, you might say—and wiped the spider (me) out.

When I began this memoir, I thought Emma had two children: my dad and Aunt Anne. Now, I know she had this son (1908), Aunt Edna/Ruth (1912), Dad (1922), Aunt Anne (1924), John (1926), and the baby she was carrying at the time of her death in 1929. Who was the father of this baby? (More on that later.) I did wonder why her parents kept the boy but put Aunt Edna/Ruth up for adoption? (Also, remember that her adoptive father also worked for the railroad.) It was shortly after the adoption that Emma married the crazy first husband (1914). There was no sign he worked for the railroad, but what about his father? It was worth checking into. More on him later as well.

I was on a roll and not about to stop. I decided I wanted to find out more about Joseph, the father of Emma's son/brother. Well, he was in all the right places in all the right time. He was a student living in the same town as Emma in 1907; the son was born in 1908, and he stayed there until 1911 when he moved to Philadelphia and married. The father suspect had six children with his first wife. She died in 1924; he married again in 1929, and through all of this, he worked for the railroad and lived in Philadelphia. Emma died in 1929 in Philadelphia. Now I know in a court of law, all this is called circumstantial evidence, but come on. How may coincidences make a reasonable conjecture? Now, I was really interested. Nancy, Aunt Edna/Ruth's niece, and I had discussed in our emails the mystery of who was the paternity of Aunt Edna/Ruth because her birth records were sealed. Could Joseph be the father of both children?

Was the father of Emma's son/brother also the father of Edna/Ruth? Why did Emma not marry the father? It was surely done in those days. Emma's parents were married on December 13 (the same date as my parents) 1888, and Emma was born eight months later—August 20, 1889. Now, a month premature is not unheard of, but in 1889, the probability of survival is significantly reduced. In 1910, Emma was listed on the census as living with her parents, her sister (age sixteen) is not on the census record, but her son/brother is. Was Edna/Ruth's birth an act of rebellion to force her parents' hand? If so, to do what? Is it significant that he is in Philadelphia when Emma died? (Hence my earlier referral to the paternity of her last child.) Were they star-crossed lovers? A fatal attraction? A modern version of Romeo and Juliet?

The other thing I must remind my readers is that in the twenty-first century, we barely blink at such a story, but in the early twentieth century, discretion was tantamount because a reputation once lost was lost forever. I think Joseph was rewarded for his discretion with a job at the railroad, but I find it curious he remained in the same town with Emma until 1911. In addition, I am beginning to see Emma's father, my great-grandfather, as heavy-handed. His position in the railroad union offered him the occasion to mix with some disreputable types. Was Pappy one of them? I will let William Shakespeare say it for me: "Oh, what a tangled web we weave when first we practice to deceive." (I could not resist the spider web reference.)

Of course, I sent this information off to Aunt Edna/Ruth's niece in California and then a follow-up email because I had to tell someone. Nancy was as surprised as I was and emailed that she was sending some new documents she discovered. One week later, I received her letter and received more startling news. Contained in the documents she sent was another certificate for a female child born to Emma and husband number one. Only this was not a birth certificate; it was a death certificate for a one-month-old female child. The cause of death was congenital syphilis, and it was signed by the same two individuals who had signed Emma's brother/son's birth certificate.

Where do I begin with all of this? One thing was settled: I knew why husband number 1 was declared insane. Insanity was a symptom of stage 3 syphilis.

> General Paresis of the Insane: This can develop anywhere between 3–30 years after initial contact with Treponema bacteria that causes Syphilis. The cranial nerves and meninges are affected and becoming inflamed. The psychiatric signs and symptoms may be deceptive, though a large part of the brain (cortex) is strongly involved. This causes significant loss of focus, memory power, and personality changes that end in insanity. Severe degeneration with permanent nervous system collapse is inevitable once General Paresis sets in. (Taken from Dove Med; http://www.dovemed.com/general-paresis-neurosyphilis)

So one thing was answered by this news. I suspect he infected her because his insanity was diagnosed during their divorce proceedings. There were no antibiotics in 1915, so the infection was spread to both Emma and their unborn child. Nancy later emailed me that, at this time, the treatment for syphilis was with mercury—good God, heavy metal poisoning!

For Emma, I wonder about her ability to have other children and her mental stability. To the best of my knowledge, my father was her next child (although I am trying to take nothing for granted at this point). My father had premature baldness and a speech stutter that was attributed to a case of spinal meningitis; he survived in 1926. But now I wonder if he survived congenital syphilis. That would mean he was infected, and I do not believe he was. He was a medical corpsman, and my mother a nurse, and believe me, she would have killed him if he were infected. They had antibiotics in 1928, but it was sometime later that their usage became widespread. Emma died in 1929, so it was too late for her.

What of Pappy? He lived until 1947, and there was no mention of similar symptoms in him. Did Pappy know about Emma's infection before they married? Of course, I wonder how she got to Philadelphia. Could she have been sent there to a sanitarium, much like TB patients were, for a cure? (Maybe, more important, away from prying eyes and waging tongues). How were her mental capabilities affected by the infection? Did she degenerate mentally as well?

Then I remembered Emma coming to me in the dream so many years ago, and I realized the significance of her attire. She came to me in a 1920s style full-length white dress—a virginal *bright* white dress. Until today, I had not thought about that dress even though it was the most vivid part of the dream because she seemed to be glowing from an internal light. I believe this is significant because despite her mortal life experiences, her attire told me that on the next plane, she had reached a place of purity and forgiveness.

I thought about how she had been separated from her children as they were scattered about. How did the birth of her son translate to the birth of her brother to friends and family? Imagine having to treat your firstborn son as your brother. Edna/Ruth went to adoptative parents. Lovely Helen died at one month of age from a sexually transmitted disease that made her father insane. My dad, who Emma cared for, suffered through an illness that nearly killed him and left him with disabilities. Anne did not even have Emma's name on her death certificate because her memory did not exist for Anne's family. John was stillborn. Baby George died with her in her womb. How much tragedy can one person absorb in forty years?

So when I thought of the dress, I derived great comfort because it represented healing for Emma. So why the nocturnal visit? Were the departed not all together on the (Paige) Cloud? Well, yes, but as I am writing this memoir, I am coming to believe that the legacy we leave in this existence is eternally important. I have not discovered the why in this, but it is on the edge of my perception. In this memoir, the memory of Emma, her children, and her grandchildren is coming together and the record corrected. I found great comfort in the thought that I played a role in this. On a practical note, I was also glad I had gotten past the feeling I needed to dig up graves and move people because this was getting really complicated.

There are so many questions for this booming bloody spider to answer. I can tell you one thing: I am getting an umbrella because the next time the blooming bloody rain comes, I want to be ready. Something tells me it better be a *big* blooming bloody umbrella so we *all* can fit under it.

Chapter 22

GOD BLESS THE USA

> I'm proud to be an American
> where at least I know I'm free,
> And I won't forget the men who died
> who gave that right to me,
> And I gladly stand up next to you
> and defend her still today,
> 'Cause there ain't no doubt I love this land
> God Bless the USA.
> (Lee Greenwood [1984], *You've Got a Good Love Comin'*)

I would guess that unless you have been in suspended animation or abducted by aliens before 1984, this lyric and melody are quite familiar to you. As seminal events occurred to and in this country, our citizens relied on it as an anthem to bolster morale and resolve. During the First Gulf War, the Iraqi War (2003), and after the attacks of September 11, 2001, this soundtrack was frequently heard in the media (Wikipedia). Just reading the lyrics brought tears to my eyes.

The time of year I write this is fall, my favorite season. The heat and humidity of the summer months are gone, leaves are turning beautiful shades of orange, red, and brown, and the harvest is all around me. My new semester has begun as has football season, and the summer hiatus is over for organizations. It is election season.

Veterans' Day is coming, and I am going to New York City to see *Hamilton* with my dear friend Jane. The fact that this musical phenomenon is occurring during all my revolutionary discoveries is not lost on me. You also need to remember that Jane was instrumental in my originals letter to the DAR, read this memoir when it was just a short story, and was my sounding board during the great George Paige debate (Is he my great-grandfather or not?). How could I ever believe in coincidence after all these events?

My deep connection to all thing's military has been thoroughly explored in previous chapters, so it is enough to just remind you that it is a seminal force in my life, and my first DAR meeting of the new year was amazing. If all of this reads like sappy, sentimental, patriotic claptrap to you, then I would like to know why you are reading this book? Spoiler alert! It is only going to get worse from here.

I am still astounded how much the DAR organization means to me. Dare I say, it has almost a spiritual experience? But remember the idea about how our behavior on this mortal plane is judged is evolving in me. I am thinking beyond the "wood, hay, and stubble" (1 Corinthians 3:11–12) that will be burned away during our accounting of this life. Based on the contents of the prior chapter, I guess this should not surprise me, but it still does. More on this theme in a minute.

As for the DAR, I have received the formal membership certificate (that I immediately took in for professional framing), and *my* affiliate greeted me as a new member. I cannot describe how that felt, and it only got better. I still find the opening ceremony very moving, and that night was no exception. During the formal meeting, I was asked to read the letter from the regent general to the group. I also received the official chapter yearbook with my name, address, membership number, and the colonel listed as my patriot. I cannot imagine life getting much better than this. I am usually a very quiet member of most groups, but here, I was looking to do more (as you will read later on, I should be careful what I wish for). There will be a formal induction ceremony at a future meeting, and all I can say is I cannot wait. I may not be able to express how I felt, but I think the colonel knew.

The lovely fall season got even better because in a month's time, I received my acceptance in the General Society of Mayflower Descendants (GSMD). I was soon off for another framing job because these certificates are official acknowledgments of all the labor, and, at times, sometimes, just plain good luck documented in this memoir. I am still trying to wrap my head around the turn of genealogical events of the past twelve months. I am really a descendant of Elder William Brewster, and this has been certified by a historian of GSMD who is just as fussy as the historian at the DAR.

When I went to the biannual GSMD meeting, with a turkey dinner, we read the Mayflower Compact, and it is all about God and country. It was hard for me to see the paper I was reading because tears kept getting in the way. Did I mention that the GSMD takes roll by ancestor? I was proud to raise my hand when William Brewster's name was read. In addition, I decided the perfect birthday gift for my son is a membership in the GSMD, and so I gathered the paperwork and submitted his application. I have a strong suspicion my grandson is next.

Now, please do not misunderstand me. I know that my heritage will mean nothing if I do not have a right relationship with God. My priorities must be right, but that being said, I am well aware that the Bible frequently shows God's preference for the descendants of His beloved like the offspring of King David. As long as a leader is human, he or she will never be perfect but imperfect; not withstanding our heritage is important. In fact, I was told by my historian colleague that I am as close to American royalty as it gets. Lest you think I am running off to have a crown made, let me assure you that I am not.

The constant flow of new information about the Paige family has slowed down to a crawl. Most of the revelations in this book occurred in the past twelve months. I am still reeling from it all and wondering if there is more to come. Now, I am not a glutton for punishment, but the adrenaline rush of the discoveries seems to be drawing down, and truth be told, I miss it some. The parts of me that loves my God and my country are grateful that both passions came together in writing this memoir. I can end this chapter where I began: God Bless the USA!

Chapter 23

THE RIVER OF DREAMS

I'm not sure about a life after this
God knows I've never been a spiritual man
Baptized by the fire, I wade into the river
That runs to the promised land
In the middle of the night
I go walking in my sleep
Through the desert of truth
To the river so deep
We all end in the ocean
We all start in the streams
We're all carried along
By the river of dreams

This chapter begins with the lyrics to *The River of Dreams* (1993) By Billy Joel. The lyric expresses skepticism about the possibility of a life after this one. I have clearly expressed my Catholic belief in this other existence. This chapter will review the writings of some individuals who do not embrace this as an unequivocal truth. You need to remember that the whole epic adventure began in part with my dream about my Grandma Emma, and so this segue is quite logical.

It is now the Christmas season, and I just finished reading several books on near-death experiences (NDE). It began one morning when I was working in the office and listening to the radio. A priest was talking about a secular book he had read and then referred the book to his father. The book was about NDE and written by an intensive care nurse in England. Now, I was always fascinated with NDEs, so I was interested, and writing this memoir acted like a catalyst for me (or more like gasoline on a fire), and I immediately ordered the book.

The Wisdom of Near-Death Experiences (2014) by Penny Sartori, PhD, is a thorough, scholarly, and readable description of NDEs and her personal research in the area. I mention this because the more I read this book, the more my dream of Emma fit the description of an NDE. There was no travel through a tunnel for me, *but* my vivid recall of the environmental details and Emma's appearance have remained the same for these thirty years. Remember when I went to Mount Moriah Cemetery to visit Pappy's grave? I was startled by the similarity of the location in the dream with the area of his burial at MMC. I learned in Dr. Sartori's book that this acuity of recall is quite unusual for a dream and made me begin to wonder about the event itself. The general rule for dreams is that if we have any recall of them as we awake, the dreams disappear like a lifting fog as we become more wakeful. I have had lots of dreams like this, but I have had a few like the dream of Emma.

This contemplation about my dream visit with Emma activated some memories for me. I do not believe I died in my sleep (yikes, at least I hope not), but I remembered that I have extremely deep dream states from time to time. I know when these events occur because the memory of the dream is crystal clear. In the morning, when I wake up, I feel like I emerged from a deep-sea dive. My dream of Emma was such a dream. I forget about these deep dream events until I have another one. Think of the irony in this. I forget about the fact that I have these deep dream states, but the memory of the dream itself remains vivid. I will make no attempt to explain the how and why of all of this; just report that I have these experiences.

My analysis is really speculation, but this whole memoir is full of speculation, so why should I stop now? I had polio at the age of two. I was in bad shape and in quarantine for seventy-two hours because polio was contagious. I have no medical records to access (they were destroyed in that darn fire because I tried to get them), and both my parents are dead, so eyewitnesses are unavailable to me. Why did this event with Emma emerge thirty years later? Remember, at the time I had *the dream*, I did not even know her last name, let alone all the discoveries I made during the writing of this memoir. I cannot answer this. I did not know how Pappy and Emma met and married, but they did, and I know they are my grandparents because of my research. I do believe in an existence beyond this life, so an experience that gives a glimpse into that life is also part of my Catholic worldview.

The other description of NDEs that rang true to me was the impact they often had on the individuals who had them (NDEers). Not all NDE experiences were positive (some NDEers thought they went to Hell), but the individuals who had a positive experience often had a renewed purpose in life because they were told they were returning to this mortal realm because *their life mission was not fulfilled*. I did not write any of the dream recollections after I read this book. As I promised in the introduction, this memoir is a journal recounting my discoveries, so there is no editing to make things line up.

Lest I forget, there was a second book I read on this topic referred to by Dr. Sartori. It was written by Ken Ebert's NDE experience titled *Theater of Clouds* (2011). How does the line in the movie *Jerry McGuire* go? "You had me at hello." How can you doubt that I would not be intrigued by the title alone? The cloud motif just keeps turning up does it not? Remember Hebrews 12:1.

The other thing I also found fascinating was that stories about NDEs can assist patients facing end of life experiences. Persons who were anxious and overwhelmed about their impending death found great comfort and peace in the NDE stories of others. Just imagine that these NDEs are so powerful that they can have a secondhand effect on other terminal patients! Dr. Sartori was very concerned however that the heavy medicating of terminal patients had the effect of blocking the NDE experience thus robbing them of the comfort of any NDE experiences either primary or secondary.

Why am I not surprised? The medical profession, for the most part, does not embrace religious beliefs and practices. It is the rare doctor who wants to hear the word *miracle*. Dr. Sartori went to some length in her book to put some distance between her research findings and religious beliefs. Because I am so familiar with research publication, I must say, in her defense, if she did not distance herself, especially from the NDEs about a Hell experience, her book would not have seen the light of day.

Because Dr. Sartori was very careful not to make a religious connection with NDEs, there is more irony because the obvious connection is a spiritual one. However, our secular media would not publish, let alone believe, her work if she did. I do not know what her personal beliefs are about NDEs, but the power of her narrative is still extraordinary even without it. After all, I became interested because a Catholic priest was recommending the book in his talk as well as recommending it to his own father. I would add the Catholic view of the communion of saints fits beautifully over her discoveries. There is a cloud of witnesses watching us (Hebrews 12:1). Why would it be so hard to believe that one or more of them would come to welcome us to the other side of this life? Or tell us that our time has not yet come because we have more to do. It takes far more mental gymnastics to stick to a secular explanation than to accept the view of the Catholic Church.

Back in chapter 2, I mentioned my tending of family graves. The Catholic Church has a long tradition of honoring the dead. The catacombs make it very clear that this belief goes back to the early Christian church. The corporal works of mercy include bury the dead (see the book of Tobit 1:17) and the spiritual works of mercy include praying for the dead. My own practice of having Masses said for the dead has expanded during this genealogical adventure to include Pappy, Emma, Aunt Anne, and the Brewster family, just to name a few. My interpretation of Emma's request to me has certainly evolved. In the beginning, my thinking was that if I found Pappy's grave, my task was over. As you and I discovered, it was just the first step in a long journey.

One other thing I added was to pick a patron saint for this book. I do not have an exhaustive knowledge of all of the saints of the Catholic Church, but I have come to respect and admire the early Church Fathers. I know about Athanasius, Irenaeus, Clement of Rome, and Justin Martyr, just to name a few. I wanted to pick someone to hold my feet to the fire and who better to do that than the irascible Saint Jerome (347–420 AD). According to *Wikipedia*, he had a focus on how a Christian woman should live her life for Christ, and of course, his most famous work was the *Vulgate*. I also know his personal foibles are very well-known, and I can relate to this. In addition, he is a Doctor of the Church, and his work is accepted by the Eastern Orthodox, Anglicans, and Lutherans, so he is ecumenical as well.

I found an interesting factoid about Saint Jerome in Bennett's (2016) book *The Apostasy that Wasn't*. At the end of his life (he died in Bethlehem), Jerome did his writing in the very cave that was venerated as the birthplace of Christ. As a Catholic Christian, I am not sure you could get any closer to true inspiration. I have added him to my daily pray list, and every night, I ask him to lead and guide this memoir (and those two worn down typing fingers) to make this book as inspirational and cogent as possible. It is my hope that he and I did exactly that. In addition, I sometimes suggest that it would be nice if he visited the (Paige) Cloud just to check on the family for me. I am sure William Brewster would love to meet him.

In this chapter, I have presented some of my speculation about my dreams with some supporting detail to show you these thoughts are more than the ravings of a baby boomer contemplating her mortality. In my Catholic Bible, Joel 3:1 reads, "Your old men shall dream dreams…" (it is Joel 2:28 in other versions). Granted I am not of the male gender but, unlike some of the more sensitive feminists, when I see the term *man,* I see it in a more global sense of God's created human race. You must admit that an author who can include Billy Joel, St. Jerome, Willian Brewster, and the communion of saints in the same chapter has a far-ranging sense of reality.

Chapter 24

AS TIME GOES BY

> It's still the same old story
> A fight for love and glory
> A case of do or die
> The world will always welcome lovers
> As time goes by
> (Herman Hupfeld [1931])

This lyric is a snippet from *As Time Goes By*. Even though this song was written during the Great Depression in the US, it is listed as one of the top tunes during the World War II era in the US. It lives forever in the movie *Casablanca* (1942) when Sam (as in *Play It Again, Sam*) accompanied himself and sang part of the lyrics. Using a lyric so deeply embedded in the WWII era was important for this chapter because a book I was reading inadvertently took me back to these significant days of my parents' adulthood.

So how did I make another discovery? It probably comes as no small surprise to you that I keep very abreast of the political world and that I love history. It all began when I happened to see a TV interview with Bret Baier who is the chief political anchor for the Fox News Channel. He had just published his book on Dwight "Ike" Eisenhower, *Three Days in January: Dwight Eisenhower's Final Mission* (2017), and he was on his book tour. (Do you see a pattern here? Once again, the trajectory of my life is altered by a media report.)

I was four years old when Ike became the thirty-fourth president of the US, so I cannot tell you that I was following election details between episodes of the *Howdy Doody Show*. There was television in those days, and I do remember Howdy Doody quite well; 1952 was also the year we left Texas, and I have already shared my recollection of seeing snow for the first time and meeting my mother's family of strangers. So even if I was a precocious four-year-old and wanted to follow Ike's election, I was facing much greater life shifts in 1952. In addition, I lost (a) Val, the Collie dog protector, (b) my home in San Antonio, (c) my military guard at Fort Sam who supported and encouraged me through my polio rehabilitation, and (d) worst of all, Dad was going far away to Europe. He was still in the army, and the army determined that his skills as a medical corpsman were needed in postwar France. I remember my mother crying, but I was so overwhelmed in my own loss; I was just four years old after all, and I had no real insight to her emotions. Her tears just meant that I was to cope with this transition and loss alone.

Remember the cigar box? It had over thirty pictures of my dad in WWII, and most of them are during R & R (as in Rest & Recreation) time on the Mediterranean. Ike was the Supreme Allied Commander in WWII. No, there are no pictures of my dad and *Ike*, but they were both part of this great world event, so they had some common experiences. The Bret Baier book has an opening chapter on Ike's military career and an overview of his command during WWII. One common circumstance for Ike and the Paige family is that we were all at Fort Sam (Houston, San Antonio, Texas) but at different times. Ike was there in 1941, my parents came later in the 1940s, and then I came along. As I read the overview of Ike's military career, several disparate pieces of information about my father's military career, which I had stored in my long-term memory, fell into place. The pieces included General Patton, North Africa, and the Battle of Anzio (Italy). I remember them the best because Dad referred to them often.

I was never sure why Dad was in North Africa. Wasn't the war in Europe and the Pacific? In reading about Ike's military career, I suddenly saw the connection. To remind you, Ike was the Supreme

Allied Commander for the Europe Command during WWII. North Africa and Italy was part of Operation Torch because the allies and Ike saw a route into Nazi-held Europe from North Africa across the Mediterranean Sea and into Italy. So Africa came first and then Italy, and suddenly, I was much clearer on what path Dad's wartime military career had taken.

There was a black-and-white movie made in 1951 titled *The Desert Fox: The Story of Rommel*. As a child, I saw the movie several years later when it was shown on TV, and Dad talked about "…chasing Rommel's Afrika Korps all over North Africa…" Dad also had grudging respect for Rommel as a military genius. At other times, he would talk about Anzio. I knew Anzio was in Italy, but I never saw the connection until I read the Baier book. In addition, Patton and the "Big Red One" were also in North Africa and Italy, so it all began to make sense, and I had a context for comments I had seen as random for all these many years. Dad was part of Patton's force. First, he was deployed to North Africa to chase Rommel. Once the Nazis were defeated, he participated in the next part of the plan to gain a beachhead in Italy.

Then there was Dad's talk of Italy and a girl during WWII-BI (before Irene). There are five pictures marked "Rita;" one picture was marked "Rita and Elenor," and one picture marked "Elenor and sisters." There was one picture marked "Frank and Rita and Elenor" and one picture masked "whole Dam family." Elenor seemed to be the common denominator in the pictures, so this was a family he knew well. I always wondered if Rita was the girl he wanted to marry, but I could not honestly say. However, if I make my judgment based on the number of pictures, then Rita wins.

Those mystery pictures began to tell a story. Dad was on the coast of the Mediterranean, and the pictures in the cigar box showed leisure times in row boats, on sandy beaches, and lots of ladies—including Rita and her whole family. Dad told us about one of these ladies because he was going to marry her. Before he could do this, his friends got him drunk, not a difficult task I think, and literally shanghaied him. When he woke up, he was on his way back to the US. Wow! Talk about a life-changing moment. After the war, Dad was given an honorable discharge and returned to Philadelphia and Pappy. Dad's intent was to work in the family business, OMG! but he and Pappy could not coexist, so Dad reenlisted. Dad was sent to Fort Sam, met my Mon, and here I am. I do have a picture from the cigar box of my dad, in uniform, and I believe he is with his intended in Europe. I did not cut her out; I just folded the picture when I put it in a frame. Now I want to go back and look at it again with new eyes. Even though my parents' relationship was less than a fairy tale romance, Mom was none too happy when mention of her came up.

This renewed interest got me to go back to the cigar box. Now I should say the box is wooden, not cardboard. The cigar brand name is *La Venga*; the type was Longfellows, and they appeared to come from Tampa, Florida (where I moved to in 2020). After checking the internet, the cigar box is considered an antique. Of course, it is less pristine because I have been dragging it around for forty years. In addition, it contained some interesting mementos from WWII. At this point, I had looked at them countless times, but I had never really *looked* at them. I also just know the contents are of the BI (before Irene) vintage.

- Four-inch triangular, khaki-colored cloth patch showing an eagle in flight and holding a swastika in its talons.
- One inch round brass-colored Caduceus uniform pin that I believe was on Dad's corpsman uniform.
- There are several old coins in the cigar box that are difficult to read; one is from Italy, and the other is what I believe to be a British halfpenny. (When I was a child, I had coins minted by the occupation forces, but those are long gone.)
- WWII sterling silver bombardier wings in mint condition (the clasp is intact and working) and it could be worth a few hundred dollars according to eBay. The Luxemburg disk is missing, but in every other respect it is the same. I have no idea where it came from. Dad was small built for a man, so maybe someone thought he would fit nicely in a bombardier bay. I can only guess how he got this because he was infantry, not a flyboy.

- A US invasion arm flag (forty-eight stars). It is four-inch wide and sixteen-and-a-half-inch long with lacing holes at either end for fitting around the upper arm. This was worn by occupying forces in Europe to make sure they were not victims of friendly fire.
- A two-inch long (sterling) metal badge, rifle in the center, blue enamel background, and laurel wreath. I am so grateful for the internet (but until today, it never occurred to me to do this inventory) because I was able to find this.

> The Combat Infantryman Badge (CIB) is a United States Army military award. The badge is awarded to infantrymen and Special Forces soldiers in the rank of colonel and below, who personally fought in active ground combat while assigned as members of either an infantry, ranger, or Special Forces unit, of brigade size or smaller, any time after 6 December 1941. (Wikipedia; https://en.wikipedia.org/wiki/Combat_Infantryman_Badge)

This is interesting because according to the Geneva Convention as a medical corpsman, Dad was a noncombat soldier, but he told me they shot at him anyway, especially at Anzio.

- WWII Purple Heart service ribbon. This one is a real mystery. Before I saved the cigar box from the trash bin, I know my mother had and sold complete sets of Dad's military uniform(s). I only ever got a glance at the footlocker that held them. Was a Purple Heart part of it? Dad was injured in Anzio, Italy. He blew out his knee jumping into a foxhole because there was no one abiding by the Geneva Convention that day.
- Two brass rifle casing that looks like it is from a 223-rifle round.

- A two-inch by four-inch membership book for Philadelphia Elks Lodge 2. I know this was Pappy's, and I am really perplexed how I lost it. I remember it well because it was the clue that led me to Mount Moriah Cemetery, but somehow, it was removed from the cigar box and never returned.
- A three-fourth by one-fourth cameo with a light brown background and a white female silhouette. It might have been part of a choker cloth necklace. There are a pair of loops on the right and left side worked into the wire-worked framing. Somehow, I always thought this was Emma's.
- There are three pictures that I am 95 percent sure are of Pappy. There is a single picture—1940s era—of a young dark-haired female that I suspect is my Aunt Anne.

I am not sure what all of this means, but I can tell you reading the Baier book really helped me to put Dad's life in context and caused me to take another look at the cigar box. After possessing it for forty years, I find it astonishing that I am just now really taking stock of its contents—me with the internet at my fingertips. Even though those pictures drove me crazy, I feel like maybe there is some context there as well.

I guess the next thing to ponder is, Why these items? The Nazi patch is the most interesting to me. Was it from a German soldier? Was he living or dead? How did Dad get it? The patch appears to have been tightly machine-stitched close to the outside edge of the patch. The only way I can see to detach it from the cloth it was sewn to would be to use something like the seam ripper I use for sewing. A razor is hard to use, and I have the cut myself often enough in this endeavor to know. I do not believe a seam ripper is standard issue for the battlefield, so I will just have to accept that the origin of this patch will just remain a mystery.

I do think I know where the cigar box came from. I think it was Pappy's. Why, you might ask? The pictures I believe I have of Pappy do seem to look like he is holding a cigar, and Dad smoked cigarettes not cigars. The box appears to have contained Cuban cigars, and for some reason, that just seems to fit Pappy. Dad could have sent the contents to him. I know their relationship was strained, but like most kids, he was looking for his father's approval. More on these musings in the next chapter.

I heard Dad talk at an AA meeting once about his relationship with Pappy. As I wrote earlier, when Dad was discharged from the army, he went home to Philadelphia and Pappy. Dad said he was expecting that his war experiences would help his father to see him as a man, but, for whatever reason, Pappy did not. (My father's illness at age four left him with a stutter, premature balding, and a 98 weakling while Pappy was somewhat athletic—a gymnast, I was told.) Pappy just saw Dad as a poor representation of a man, and I think Dad was an embarrassment to Pappy. Dad wanted to work with Pappy in the family business—a night club, Dad said. It did not work, and Dad reenlisted in the army and on to Fort Sam.

I just think Dad found the cigar box when he returned to Philadelphia for Pappy's funeral. The cigar box was left with Pappy when Dad reenlisted, and Dad discovered it with Pappy's personal effects when Dad went home for the funeral in 1947. The pictures might have been sent to Pappy to show him Dad's European deployment. I have another reason for this belief because of the framed poem and picture that was in the box. But that is a topic for the next chapter of this memoir.

Back to the World War II ruminations, I had one other realization about myself because I read the Baier book. When I was reading about Ike's second term in 1956, when I was eight years old, I knew that his Democratic opponent was Adlai Stevenson. I remembered that because I knew it in 1956. Now, think about this for a minute. That is a clear indicator how deeply politics was part of our household. I remember wearing an "I Like Ike" lapel button and making jokes about how much golf he played, and I was eight years old! Our household was not too deeply divided politically yet because Dad was just back for good from the army, and alcohol took up most of his time and thinking. I think Mom, the Democrat, could not say too much against Ike because she was a military veteran, and Ike had hero status in 1956.

"As Time Goes By" fits this chapter on so many levels. I have had the cigar box for forty years, and I have just now examined the box itself and the physical contents more closely. Dad has been gone for forty years, and I have suddenly made sense of some important details of his life. That song and lyric are classic, and much like this story, they emerge from time to time and make connections with many generations. Like Humphrey Bogart's famous line, *Play It Again, Sam*, the cigar box required many return trips to examine the contents as time went by. Who knows what I will find the next time I look?

Chapter 25

IN MY LIFE

> There are places I'll remember
> All my life, though some have changed.
> Some forever, not for better;
> Some have gone and some remain.
> All these places had their moments
> With lovers and friends I still can recall.
> Some are dead and some are living,
> In my life I've loved them all.
> But of all these friends and lovers
> There is no one compares with you.
> And these mem'ries lose their meaning
> When I think of love as something new

Now I must admit to extreme prejudice in the selection of this lyric. I have included more lines of this lyric than any other cited in this memoir. It is from my favorite group: the Beatles. It was written by John Lennon and Paul McCarthy. (A little trivia for you—it is also classified as Baroque Rock because there is a harpsichord in the foreground of the music; who knew? [https://en.wikipedia.org/wiki/In_My_Life]). It is from my favorite Beatles album, *Rubber Soul* (1965), and it is among my favorite cuts from the album. I am happy I got to use it in this memoir. It also really captures the essence of this chapter as we continue to examine the contents of the cigar box.

I will begin by saying that today is the seventieth anniversary of Pappy's death. I attended Mass this morning, and the Mass intention was for Pappy. I know I have written in prior chapters that I sometimes feel Pappy's presence with me, particularly in the kitchen. When I make hash brown potatoes, I just feel like Pappy is looking over my shoulder to check out my recipe and technique. I suppose a fitting end to this day would be for me to make hash browns for dinner tonight (and I did). At any rate, I just felt like Pappy was at Mass with me this morning, and dare I say, he imparted a feeling of gratitude to me for the offered prayers. I will venture even farther because I felt like he was happy to have me as his granddaughter and saw me as one of his son's more successful contributions to the Paige family. This was such a healing thought for me because I know of all the angst that existed between Dad and Pappy. The feelings are not without great irony for me.

I have written about my trip to Mount Moriah Cemetery to pay my respects to Pappy and leave a flower memorial. While I was there, I had such a strong sense of my father standing next to Pappy's open grave, on an March day, and being so conflicted by the depth of his loss. They never got along, so why should Dad feel like this? Even Mount Moriah had a sense of *déjà vu* because it looked amazingly like the site of my nocturnal visit from Grandma Emma. I have related all of these events in this memoir, but only just now am I beginning to feel how interrelated these events are and in the center of it all is the cigar box.

I am now about 95 percent sure the cigar box first belonged to Pappy. Remember, Aunt Anne's birth certificate was in the box. Why would Dad have that? The cameo, the pictures of Pappy and who I believe to be Aunt Anne, the Elks Club membership manual, and my belief that Pappy liked his cigars (and my Dad did not) support my conclusion. I think that forty years ago, Dad found this box while he was going through Pappy's effects. From that moment on, it became Dad's cigar box. He could have thrown it away but he did not. I believed he kept it because it was a connection to Pappy and a reminder of his love of cigars—smell and all?

THE SOUNDTRACK OF MY LIFE

There has been an enigma surrounding the box from the beginning of my examinations. I thought I knew what it was forty years ago, but today, all new alternatives have captured my mind. There is a framed picture of a poem, clipped from the newspaper, and a picture of a young boy. The metal picture frame is 4 1/2" x 6 1/2" and a tarnished gold color. There is a 1 1/2" x 2 3/4" black-and-white picture of a young boy who appears to be about four years old. The child is looking off to his left, so the face is a profile. He is outdoors, on a lawn, with a brick house close behind him. He has thick dark hair; he is wearing short pants (or possibly a kilt) and with a white shirt with three-fourth sleeves.

Next to the picture is a typeset poem on old, yellowed newsprint titled, "To My Son." Being the good academic that I am, I looked for the verse, doing an internet search, and I could not find it. Therefore, I cannot cite the author GTS. The poem reads as follows:

> Here's to you, my son, whom I love as you should never know.
> To you, my boy, who is to take my place when it's time for me to go?
> I've wondered what type of chap you would be, and I've wished I could take your hand.
> Just to whisper "I wish you well my boy" in a way you'd understand.
> I'd like to give you a cheering word, that I've longed at time to hear,
> I'd like to give you the warm hand clasp, when never a friend seemed near.
> I've learned my knowledge through sheer hard work, and I wish I could pass it on
> To you, who will take my place, some day when I am gone?
> The galley cup, the bitter pang, the road I've trod alone,
> The harvest you shall reap from the seed I have sown.

> Will you see all the sad mistakes I made and note all the battles lost?
> Will you ever guess the tears they have caused, or the heartaches they cost?
> Will you gave [sic] through the failure and fruitless toil of the underlying plan,
> And catch a glimpse of a real intent of the heart of the vanished man?
> I may dare to hope you may pause someday, as you toil as I have wrought
> And gain some strength for your weary task, from the battles I have fought.
> But I've only the task itself to leave, with the cares for you to face,
> And never a cheering word may speak to you, who will take my place.
> Then here's to your health, my boy, I drink as a bridegroom to a bride
> I leave an unfinished task for you, but God knows how I tried
> I've dreamed my dreams as all men do, but very few came true.
> And my prayer today is that all of my dreams maybe realized by you.
> And we'll meet someday in the Great Unknown out in the realms of space,
> And you'll know my clasp as you take my hand, and gaze into your tired face.
> Then all our failures will be success in the light of the newfound dawn,
> So here's to you, my boy, who will take my place when I'm gone.
>
> (G.T.S.)

Remember Emma died when Dad was almost seven years old? For many years, I assumed the picture was of my pre-meningitis

Dad, and the poem was from Emma. I had read the poem in the past, but the act of transcribing it for this memoir forced closer attention. The sentiment is clear. It seems to be a male parent making an adieu to their male child. Remember, Dad's illness left him with physical changes when he was four, and Emma died when he was seven. What bothered me about this thought was Emma's death seemed to be accidental even though it was a septic infection from a self-inflicted wound. I never had the sense that Emma intended to kill herself, but she picked a very dangerous way to escape a difficult situation.

Then a thought occurred to me. Did this memento predate my father? Was it a remnant from Emma referring to her firstborn son Kenneth? Remember, Kenneth, Emma's first child, was raised as her brother. It is clear in the words that there is regret about a future that will not be shared. In addition, I have more unanswered questions to add to the pile. Who is the GTS that is cited as the author? What newspaper was this taken from? Did the cigar box come to Pappy from Emma?

There is another picture in the cigar box of a young man, maybe twenty years old and blond, down on all fours with a child "riding" on his back. For whatever reason, I thought the man was Emma's brother John Jr. In addition, the child on his back looks similar (Or is it wishful thinking on my part?) to the child in the framed picture. So is the photo of my Great Uncle John having a playful moment with his nephew/brother Kenneth? Or my Dad?

The sentiment expressed in the poem has youthful tone of regret and lost opportunities. By the time my father was born and had his meningitis, Emma had given birth to Uncle Kenneth (raised as her brother), Aunt Edna/Ruth (given up for adoption), Aunt Helen (died at one month from syphilis), Dad (born 1922), Aunt Anne (born in 1924), and Uncle John (stillborn in 1926). (These are the ones I have discovered.) I think the reality of life would have set in by 1926–29, and her view about leaving an unknown offspring would have been more jaded—more John Doe, I think. I suppose this is just another thing I will not know for sure in this side of eternity, but it lends support to the belief that the cigar box might have come to Pappy via Emma.

There is one other way to look at the source of this memento. Was the voice male because it represented the sentiments of Pappy grieving over his son John who was stillborn? Pappy made no secret of his embarrassment over my dad's physical appearance and speech impediment (and I am sure, later, by Dad's alcoholism). Perhaps John's death was a great letdown because Pappy's dreams of a *real man* to carry on the family name were dashed. Because I know this animosity existed between Dad and Pappy, my feelings at Mass today were significant.

In this life, Dad could not live up to Pappy's expectations of manhood. On top of that, Dad's firstborn, me, has a physical disability (as does my brother with his cross-eye). In Pappy's worldview, none of us portray the sterling examples he would choose to carry on the family name. However, in the next life, where the long game is crystal clear, gratitude and reconciliation are possible when small mercies are received. I believe Pappy came to see a book should not be judged by its cover. Today's graces, for the Mass and prayers and Pappy's gratitude, were very affirming to me because I knew it meant he saw Dad and I in a whole new light.

As I am typing this, Pappy's death certificate is lying on the desk in front of me. My father provided the information, and disinformation, on this document. I just noticed that Dad listed his home address as the same address of the funeral home that took care of Pappy's burial plans. Dad was in Philadelphia from Fort Sam, so this seems like an odd choice to make. Why not list Fort Sam as his home address? He was dating my mom at this time, and in less than nine months, they would be married, and I would be on the way. I guess I have another thing to add to my list of clarifications when Dad and I are reunited one day.

At this moment, I am not sure if I have clarified these genealogical things or muddied the water so much I will never untangle the whole thing. Grandma Emma's directions to me were to bring the family together, and this morning in church, I had the impression that I had done a small bit of this between Dad and Pappy. I must admit the knowledge of this makes me feel pretty good. Now the day would be perfect if Pappy could tell me how he got from Vermont to

Ohio and then to Philadelphia, but I guess I am just getting greedy for information. I will say I suspect the railroad has something to do with it because of Emma's father, Grandpa John, who was a big shot in the Pennsylvania Railroad union. In addition, I would really like to know who raised Pappy because Great-Granddad George did not seem to have done so. The family was all in Vermont, so Pappy's getting to Ohio was a real mystery but I guess a mystery for another day.

Today has been eventful, and my chosen song lyric fits perfectly. "Some are dead and some are living, in my life I've loved them all…" I can honestly say that over these years, since I went to Mount Mariah, I have come to know Pappy better, and dare I say, I have come to love him. Neither he nor I would have selected each other, but in the grand scheme of things, Pappy is as perfect for me as I am for him. I know I would be happy to know that in seventy years, when I am gone from this world, someone would keep my memory alive and take the time to pray for my immortal soul. All I can say to this idea is "amen."

Chapter 26

ONE OF US

> If God had a face, what would it look like?
> And would you want to see?
> If seeing meant that you would have to believe
> In things like Heaven and in Jesus and the saints
>   and all the prophets?
> And yeah, yeah God is great
> Yeah, yeah, God is good
> Yeah, yeah, yeah, yeah, yeah

"One of Us" is a song written by Eric Bazilian (of The Hooters) and originally released by Joan Osborne in March 1995 on the album *Relish* (wikipedia.com). I love this song, and I love Joan Osborne. My son owned the *Relish* CD, and we were always asking one another to have it back so we could listen to it. I was captivated by both the lyrics and the music.

Some folks are bothered by the line, "What if God was one of us. Just a slob like one of us…" Referring to the Incarnation of the God-Man as a slob might be a bit beyond respectful. However, I recommend you read Philippians 2:6–7: "Who though he was in the form of God, did not regard equality with God something to be grasped. Rather he emptied himself, taking the form of a slave, coming in human likeness…" This passage compares the Incarnation to becoming a slave—a human slave. This is a point to ponder because there are higher classes of humanity, and yet the lowest form was freely taken by Jesus. Perhaps the term slob is harsh, but I think there is some equivalency.

So why this lyric? Well, after twenty years, I have my own Joan Osborn CD. My son finally gave me the original, but it is scratched and plays poorly, so I bought a compilation CD. I found it in my car the other day and realized I had not listened to it for a while. As I was driving and singing along, I wondered how I could write this memoir without including this lyric. Then I had another dilemma: I cannot just create the chapter to include the lyric. However, as I thought about recent events, I realized that I had been contemplating my next step in this memoir, and this lyric fits quite nicely.

To begin with, I have been quite clear about my Catholic belief in the communion of saints, so seeing the face of God fits in with my ancestors' experiences. In the previous chapter, I wrote about my experiences at the seventieth anniversary Mass of Pappy's death, and since then, I also had the fortieth anniversary Mass for Dad. In addition, I also obtained a wonderful DVD about Purgatory (*Purgatory: The Forgotten Church*). In that DVD, a priest described a feeling of *gratitude* from the souls for whom he offers prayers. I used that exact word in the previous chapter when I described how I felt at Pappy's anniversary Mass (*and* I wrote that before I saw the DVD). I believe this brings another layer of understanding to Grandma Emma's directive to me. I believe the growing connection between those of us living with those of us who have moved on to another existence is very important, and seeing the face of God is no small part of this experience.

Being Roman Catholic also helps me to go beyond the linear time frame we are locked into in this life. God exists outside of the succession of time. God was kind enough to explain in Genesis His creation of the world in seven linear days because we live in this time frame. I was able to put myself at Pappy's bedside, praying the chaplet of Divine Mercy, while he was dying because I know God is not limited by our time restrictions. I cannot move myself back in time; however, I can ask God to receive my prayers and place them at the right time and place. At every Mass we attend, there is a suspension of linear time as the priest, in the person of Christ (in *persona Christi*), unites himself with Jesus and the sacrifice on Calvary. Lest you think this notion of the timeless nature of God is a new idea, we can go back to St. Augustine (fifth century) to find this notion. As for me, I cannot explain exactly how this works, but I accepted it in faith and prayed accordingly. I have learned that these family connections are much stronger than I ever realized.

In a prior chapter, I wrote about my fascination with the TLC series, *Who Do You Think You Are?* Well, to give an indication about the linear time span, I have been working on this memoir when the next season of this series just ended. Liv Tyler, daughter of rocker Steven Tyler (Aerosmith), was the focus on an episode. She discovered that she and her father had an ancestor who was a former slave and then indentured servant. He was listed as mulatto on early census records, but eventually, he passed for white, and he was a drummer. When Stephen Tyler, who began his music career as a drummer, found out, he said he just always knew about his ancestry—just like I always knew that I had Jewish ancestry. In every case, when individuals discovered their ancestry, they felt an immediate connection and wanted to go to see the place their ancestor lived and worked—like I did when I went to Mount Moriah to Pappy's grave. When I began this search, I had no idea how deeply those family connections go, but Grandma Emma sure did, and I believe seeing the face of God was the catalyst.

In addition, this discovery also shows yet again the wisdom and correctness of the Catholic Church. Death does not cut us off from our loved ones. We may not have the physical presence of a loved one, but the spiritual connection, as I have learned through this process, can be quite strong. I just heard a story on EWTN of a man whose dead son came to him in a vivid dream (Seeing any similarities here?) who told his father he was fine. The son was worried about his grieving Dad who was being torn up by the son's death. The dad is now a father (priest) in the Catholic Church. I love the synchronicity of it all.

The other thing I viewed on EWTN was an interview with Father Kevin McGoldrick (May 30, 2017) who was a musician and, a later vocation, as a Catholic priest. In his interview, he talked about *twisted mystics*. He used this term to describe secular musicians who write music and lyrics that have a deep spiritual message. For the most part, this is not a conscious choice on their part. Truth is truth, and music is a powerful medium by which to transmit messages and to praise the God of the universe—whether a musician/lyricist is intentional or not.

In my perspective, music becomes a two-edged sword however:

1. On one hand, music has a powerful influence on our emotions. Just think of the "love songs," the "she/he doesn't love me anymore" songs, and the "will anybody love me" songs, just to name a few. Then those themes are embedded in a melody of the blues, rap, country, classical, pop, or jazz.
2. Music has the power to elicit memories. While I was playing Joan Osborne, I was carried back to my life in 1995—where I was and what I was doing.
3. Music can be and is used in propaganda, advertising, political campaigns, and in any other means possible to influence and actually control human behavior. It can entertain us, sooth us (like King Saul and the songs of David in the Old Testament), divert us, and convince us. It is such a subtle form of influence that most of us do not often realize what is happening to us. Our minds are quite susceptible to subliminal suggestions, and music is an excellent delivery system for this weapon.

I must admit I was glad to hear about *twisted mystics*. In case you have not noticed, this memoir gives a significant amount of space to music and lyrics. I had some concern that my chapters did not all begin with hymn lyrics. After all, I am telling my genealogy story from a Roman Catholic perspective. Then I heard Father Kevin and realized secular does not necessarily equate to bad or unacceptable. However, I am not suggesting that the music and lyrics selected here are all of the virtuous variety.

"Helter Skelter," for example, is more about ugly chaos rather than order and natural beauty because that chapter is all about the chaos I was feeling at that point of my genealogical search. Why do movies have soundtracks (or my life for that matter)? How evil and oppressive would Darth Vader be without the iconic John Williams' Imperial March that announces his presence? What would Freddie Krueger or Michael Meyers be without gripping and suspenseful background music? Then there is the shark by which all other sharks are measured and that slow but building melody that announces the presence of Jaws. James Bond, 007, is a very iconic character, but no matter what actor plays that part, the theme music is the common theme that creates a long cannon of movie scripts and characters. Then there is the earworm—a <u>catchy</u> piece of music that continually repeats through a person's mind after it is no longer playing (wikipedia.com). The earworm can be pleasing, but it can also be very annoying (and advertises do not really care if they annoy you because they have you thinking about them either way).

I think I built my case for the role of music in our lives and the importance of it in this memoir. Additionally, I have realized that secular music need not be ignored in this endeavor. The lyrics to "One of Us" asks some pretty direct questions for a popular secular song in 1995. If you see the face of God, will you believe in Heaven? Jesus? The saints? All the prophets? It is my belief that all of these persons exist and, of course, The (Paige) Cloud is located in Heaven. I must admit that I did not really see all of this when I began this process. The song lyrics just seemed like a good idea in the beginning of this memoir, but I could not have explicitly told you why it was a good idea, but now, I can.

I believe Joan Osborn and/or Eric Bazilian, the lyricist, are twisted mystics. The questions they ask in this lyric are direct and unequivocal. If you could see the face of God, would you want to if seeing Him meant you had to believe? How many people who say, "Yeah I believe in God" would answer yes that they want to see God let alone have to believe in Him, Jesus, the saints, and all the prophets and, yikes, the Ten Commandments?

I guess the point is that the connection to the communion of saints must go through a personal God, a personal Savior, and done on God's terms, not ours. I believe spiritualists try to cut out the middleman. They want the connection without the hierarchy—medium and séances without rules and accountability. In the Old Testament, King Saul found out in 1 Samuel 28:7–19 as he violated his own edict and used a medium to conjure up Samuel the prophet. The news was not good for Saul because Samuel told him that he and his sons would all be dead the next day.

So the reality is, a spiritual connection can be made Saul's way, but it violates rules that are so primal it is done at great risk. "But seek first the kingdom [and face] of God, and His righteousness, and all these things will be given to you besides" (Matthew 6:33). To me, the height of pride is to think we can create our own rules to navigate a universe we did not create let alone comprehend in its vastness and complexity. This is much the same as Emma's "bring us together" directive to me. I have learned through all of this that I had no idea what she meant or even what is possible and that my learning has only just begun.

Chapter 27

LIFE IS A HIGHWAY

Life's like a road that you travel on
When there's one day here and the next day gone
Sometimes you bend and sometimes you stand
Sometimes you turn your back to the wind
There's a world outside every darkened door
Where blues won't haunt you anymore
Where the brave are free and lovers soar
Come ride with me to the distant shore
We won't hesitate
To break down the garden gate
There's not much time left today
Life is a highway
I wanna ride it all night long
If you're going my way
I wanna drive it all night long

"Life Is a Highway" was written by Tom Cochrane and recorded on his album *Mad, Mad World* in 1991. In addition, it has also been covered by a number of artists (wikipedia.com). I would suggest that Tom Cochrane is a *twisted mystic*. The truth of these lyrics is rarely disputed and a wonderful metaphor for our human existence. Life never proceeds in a straight line, and try though we may, we are not going to control the highway conditions. We can select a route and a destination, but then the only thing in our human hands is how we are going to deal with the accidents, detours, breakdowns, and inclement weather (aka storms) we encounter. The circuitous path documented in this memoir is a testament to this reality. One of the reasons I write this memoir is because I know most people can relate to my experience, and the rest of you are in denial.

The perfect life and the perfect family only exist on TV, and TV is fiction—even reality TV. I will be the first to admit that my genealogical discoveries uncovered some individuals who I am proud to declare as my ancestors. The colonel, the captain, and William Brewster immediately come to mind. But then there is my Pappy with his connections to some questionable (aka criminal) individuals like his boss (who in case you do not remember was murdered with a baseball bat and/or a pipe). Grandma Emma seemed to begin a promising life, but at thirty-nine years of age, she was dead, under questionable circumstance, and having birthed seven children (and those are the ones who I have discovered; there could be more) by three or four fathers. My own parents battled alcoholism, and it seems the demon drink saturated much of my family history. Truth be told, my positive ancestry discoveries were far more surprising than if I had discovered an axe murder or two. I spent most of my life thinking I was of Irish and Polish descent. I embraced that identity only to find out I am not Irish at all, and there is some Jewish and Russian mixed in with the Polish. (Culture is more about ideas and attitudes than biology, but that is another book.)

The other idea in the lyric is that we meet people on the road of life and share parts of the journey with them. This can include spouses, friends, and professional/business relationships. Some of our pairings can be a personal choice, but I believe most of our pairings/groupings are out of our hands. This should come as no small surprise to the readers. I do not believe in coincidences because I believe in God. He knows there are some people I would avoid like the plague, and so He puts them in my classes, my church, my neighborhood, and on the road with me. Who more than our family fits this category? "You can pick your friends but not your relatives" is so cliché it bears no further explanation to you. I am sure Pappy clearly would have not picked Dad or me to be his progeny, yet I recently experienced his gratitude with both Dad and I at his memorial Mass. So the lyric describes our trip to the "distant shore" on the highway of life, and this journey is full of twists and turns, wind and dark, and the blues and changing scenery. As you have been reading this memoir, it is quite clear that is very descriptive of my own journey.

Now I need to be honest. I thought my last chapter was the end of this memoir. Because life is such a journey, at some point, I am going to need to determine enough is enough and just stop writing and return to my other life activities but not just yet. My story just rolled on to a new event, and I had the perfect lyric, so I am still writing. However, you need some context for this part of my memoir, so I need to digress a bit.

This part of the story predates all my genealogical endeavors and has to do with highways and how I travel them. I always buy new SUVs. An SUV is easier for me to get into and out of and easily accommodates my disassembled scooter. A used car is for someone who can fix and/or repair the vehicle or knows someone who can fix and/or repair a vehicle, and I am neither of these persons. With a new car, I pay a lower interest rate, I never buy new tires (except the time I had a sidewall mishap), and the car is gone before the warranty is up.

I am literally the little old lady who drives four miles per day to work and/or church, and most of the time, I usually trade in a car that is three years old and has approximately 20,000 miles on it. I swear there are folks following me into the dealership when I trade in a car. Since 1992, I have owned approximately eight new cars. Car salesmen love me because I come in with the necessary paperwork, and I talk money before any test drives—no use getting attached to a vehicle I cannot afford. I always buy American vehicles. I have been told that it makes no difference because many parts are imported. I buy the name on the vehicle, and having read my history, this buying preference should come as no surprise. The first car I drove and the first cars I owned were made by American Motors Corporation (AMC).

About fifteen years ago, I had a close acquaintance with a Jeep Wrangler, and I loved driving it and riding in it. (By the way, in

1970, Jeep became part of AMC. The Jeep/Eagle division of Chrysler Corporation was formed from the AMC Jeep Renault dealer network. It was in fact the Jeep line that kept AMC going until the mid-1980s [Wikipedia].) It was made even better because the Jeep is quintessentially American. It was developed first for the military in 1941 and World War II. When I think of Ike, I see him in my mind's eye in his military uniform and sitting in a Jeep. If that is not enough, while I was in the heat of my DAR genealogical discoveries for the colonel, I parked next to a Jeep, and the model's name, Patriot, was emblazoned on the side. The idea of owning a Jeep took on a new dimension beyond its connection to AMC, that it was an American car manufacturer (despite the Fiat ownership), and the military history attached to it only added intensity to my desire to own a Jeep. It became a statement vehicle for me—a patriot.

In addition, I was ending my second year on my current vehicle when, suddenly, I was surrounded by Jeeps of all sizes and colors. If I saw five cars, three of them were Jeeps. I could be driving down the road, and there would be a Jeep in front of me, a Jeep behind me, and a Jeep passing me. It appears I had a kind of Jeep radar. It was not that there were more Jeeps; it was just like my attention was diverted to all the Jeeps in my vicinity. This went on for a couple of months. It was not annoying as much as it was hard to ignore. I was not ready to buy, but I have learned not to ignore these kinds of circumstances, and as I wrote, I do not believe in coincidences. I took to the internet and worked on the Jeep site, and lo and behold, the Patriot 4x4 was in my price range. Through the wonders of the internet, I had access to look at the vehicle sticker. I found the vehicle in the color I wanted, Mojave Sand, and the only dealer that had two in stock.

For one reason or another, my desire and my actual ownership of a Jeep never seemed to come together. For a while, I was warned about transmission issues that seemed to come with the Jeep-Chrysler merger. Fast forward to a few weeks ago, I was with my son and his father-in-law (a retired master auto mechanic), and I again mentioned my desire to own a Jeep but that I was still hesitant because of mechanical issues. He assured me that there were no problems like this now; he currently owns two Chrysler products since

Fiat bought Chrysler. When it comes to things mechanical, his pronouncements are simply accepted as the ultimate and final authority, so another barrier was gone.

I put this Jeep idea aside to allow it to percolate for a while. I even put the piece of paper with the vehicle info in my small corner shrine with the Blessed Mother and Saint Joseph and asked for guidance. A day later, I was watching a TV series show, and one of the commercials was, "If you want a Jeep, buy a Jeep." Goodness, this was getting ridiculous. The next day, I called the insurance company, and because I had the VIN number from the internet, I found out my insurance would increase $1 per month. Did you hear that barrier drop? There was only one way to settle this. I drove to the dealer to talk money. If the money did not add up, then it was done with for now.

The dealership was quiet when I came in on my crutches. I just had the sense I did not look like a hot prospect to the sales staff, so no one rushed to my assistance. When Bob asked me, "Can I help you?" I told him I wanted to talk to a salesman, and he walked me over to his desk. I kind of surprised him because when he wanted to check his inventory for a vehicle, I gave him the VIN for the car I wanted, my current car loan information, title to my car, and insurance information. I told him it was necessary to discuss money first because I already knew I wanted a Jeep, but I was not driving something out of my price range.

As we chatted, I told him about the TV commercial that gave me the nudge to come to the dealership. He asked what show I was watching, and I told him. He visits with his mother on Sunday (did I tell you he is Polish?), and they watch this same show, their favorite show, together. In addition, my name is the same name as one of the main characters on the show, and so he said, "This was meant to be." Now I realize he is a car salesman—but at least not a *used* car salesman—so a grain or two of salt may be called for here. I will say I know he watches the show because we digressed into several minutes of discussion about detailed plot developments.

When we returned to the mathematics of the visit, the payment went up but within reason, so I decided I could make a test drive. It was love at first sight because, remember, it was all about the color. The final barrier crumbled like Mojave Sand in the wind. I should also add that the morning Mass the day I picked up the vehicle was for my father's sister Anne, another ancestor of the colonel. (I had scheduled the Mass a year before, so I did not even remember until Father read the Mass intention that morning). If I was on a literal highway, I would surely see all these sign as indicators I was on the right road.

Now you are wondering why I take the time to write about my quirky car buying behavior. Two days before I made the deal to buy the car, I was sworn in as the vice-regent for my DAR group. One and a half years ago, I knew nothing about DAR membership, and now they were making me an officer. In two years' time, I can ascend to the role of regent if I navigate the vice-regent role carefully. My dear friend Jane, mentioned earlier in this memoir, is also joining my DAR chapter. All of this happened because, in 1977, I took the life-changing action of asking for and looking into the cigar box containing my father's personal effects. If not for that, I would still think I was an Irish/Polish-American and be wondering how many alcoholics and ax murders I had in the family.

This Jeep was more than just another vehicle. If one can make a statement with their vehicle, I want to with mine because it represents things that I value. (I also have a rosary and the Sacred Heart prominently displayed.) I cannot think of a better vehicle for me—a Jeep Patriot. I know I am talking about a car, a thing, and in the greater scheme of things, I will not be driving it, or any vehicle, to the pearly gates and my encounter with God. Neither am I trying to make an argument for material possessions being the be all and end all of this life. However, I will be traveling down life's highway, for as long as the Lord allows, so why not as Catholic, a proud American patriot, and an officer in the DAR. I cannot think of a better way for me to travel toward the distant shore.

By the way, I should also add that the first thing everyone comments on when they first see the car goes something like, "I like/love the color."

Chapter 28

WE ARE THE CHAMPIONS: PART 2

I've paid my dues
Time after time
I've done my sentence
But committed no crime
And bad mistakes
I've made a few
I've had my share of sand kicked in my face
But I've come through
(And we mean to go on and on and on and on)
We are the champions my friends
And we'll keep on fightin' till the end
We are the champions
We are the champions
No time for losers
'Cause we are the champions
Of the world
(Freddie Mercury [1977], *News of the World*)

Unless you have lived a hermit's existence, these lyrics and melody should be very familiar to you. "We Are the Champions" is the anthem often played when one of America's professional sports teams becomes the world champion of their sport, and yes, I used this for chapter 20. I like the lyrics because they are gritty and realistic, and I think Freddie Mercury could be considered a *twisted mystic*. The *champion* portrayed here was bloody, bruised, and beaten but also resilient and persistent to the completion of their task. The essential question then is, "Is it worth it?"

As for sports championships, human success is often very fleeting, and as proof, I ask you to research the end of some of these "champions" (i.e., Tiger Woods). The definition of a champion is "a person who has defeated all opponents in a competition or series of competitions, so as to hold first place" (dictionary.com). Based on this definition, I believe Jesus was a true champion when he uttered, "It is finished" from the cross on Calvary. In defeating sin, death, and Satan, Jesus gave everything He had. In addition, His death was anything but noble. Dying on a cross was considered a curse ("For he who is hanged is cursed by God…" [Deuteronomy 21:23]) and was the lowest form of execution. He was crucified between two common criminals. During the public three hours on the cross, Jesus was naked—a grave humiliation for a Jew. He was beaten beyond human recognition. He was mocked by the Roman soldiers, the passersby, the spectators, and one of the criminals. The only variation from our lyric is that Jesus made *no* bad mistakes; He made no mistakes. Jesus told His followers they would have to follow His example, so if we pick up our cross to follow Him, the lyrics describe us perfectly (Matthew 16: 24). Life is difficult; our successes are often not pretty or even obvious, and we emerge from them looking much the worse for wear. However faithful persistence, not style points, are the real measure of success in God's eyes.

I am not alone in using sports analogies to make a point about the spiritual realm. St. Paul did it quite a bit (1 Corinthians 1:25, 9:24–27; 1 Timothy 6: 11–12; 2 Timothy 2:5). From a Catholic Christian's perspective, the Bible is full of scripture references about perseverance/endurance (Romans 5:2–5; 2 Corinthians 3–10; Jam 1:2–4, 1:12; Hebrews 12:1–2). Jesus was very clear about the result of our persistence (John 14:2). Why do we do it? The rewards are great, but the journey is guaranteed to be difficult (John 13:16).

Why do we get out of bed in the morning? I believe another metaphor will help here.

Life is like an onion. It makes you shed tears when you remove the papery skin, when you slice and dice it, and when heat is added to sauté. I am not sure what prompted the first humans to think onions might be good to eat. I do know there are individuals who eat a plain raw onion. They do not cook it or dice/slice it raw to add to other foods but consume it in its simple eye-watering glory. However, I would suggest these folks are a very small minority because the aroma of raw onions does not permeate the atmosphere around us, at least in America. I return to wondering why anyone thought onions were good to eat. I am equally surprised to learn that a gently sautéed or deep-fried onion can be sweet to the taste. When preparing dinner, the onion is not the main course, but it certainly makes the main course more savory.

Why is life like this? When looking at basic human existence, there does not appear to be a lot to be optimistic about. There are diseases, poverty, violence, famine, weather extremes, and evil, just to name a few of the barriers faced by humankind. It would seem persistence/endurance is essential for basic survival let alone the quality of our spiritual life. It reminds me of the Peggy Lee song, "Is That All There is?" (See chapter 18). If you have read this entire memoir, you know I have had some experience with barriers, and so I have some authority in commenting on attempts to overcome them. But I ask you to think it though. When does a meal taste the best? When you are hungry. (My mother always said when you are hungry, you will always eat what is put in front of you.) When does a glass of cold water taste like ambrosia? When you are thirsty from work and exertion right? Just like the onion, difficulty makes life's success more savory and, with enough heat, even sweet.

Polio was an awful experience, but it did not kill me. In retrospect, I can attribute many positive life experiences (like completing my PhD) that had their genesis in my polio experience. I would not have chosen polio to be a defining life experience any more than I would choose raw onions as the main staple of my diet. However, at this very moment, as I am typing this memoir (with my two fingers),

I am aware of the aftereffects (some pain and mobility issues, just to name a few) of my polio virus. Yet I continue to type and move on to complete the day ahead of me. Like the onion, the physical effort may make me cry, but it does not stop me from plotting my course for tomorrow.

I have a perfect example of this. Beyond polio, the mental effects of aging are a concern for me. When I cannot find my car keys, if I forget a name and/or a life incident, my first thought is, "Dementia is beginning!" The other day, I visited a dear friend in an assisted living facility. This is a rather upscale place, and the residents are college educated professionals. The environment is very comfortable with lots of amenities. However, it did not take me long to feel an atmosphere of malaise. It was a slow shuffling kind of thinking that accompanied all the human operators of scooters, walkers, and canes. It became crystal clear to me when I stayed for a cultural event—a slide show about a local historical site renovation. I felt incandescent in that room while the lady next to me dozed off during the presentation. It was crystal clear to me that all of my daily life challenges in keeping my house, doing my job, and participating in social commitments, in spite of my polio, were my onions. It kept my brain sharp, and it made me realize that lessening responsibility for seniors may not be doing them any favors.

So what is the point of all this talk of onions, champions, and persistence? Throughout this memoir, I have recounted my growing realization that Grandma Emma was not asking me to exhume her or any other family members. (However, my concern about the rental cost of a bulldozer should give you an insight at how literal I can be.) In addition, right from the beginning of this memoir, I was clear about my belief in the communion of saints. I now realize my belief was based more on my faith in Catholic doctrine than personal life experiences. There is nothing wrong with this because faith, by definition, is based on mental acceptance more than concrete proof. Faith is defined as "confidence or trust in a person or thing: belief that is not based on proof" (dictionary.com). The point is that this genealogical experience enriched my understanding of the communion of saints and just how important knowing family history/stories really is.

The first thing I now understand much better is just how subjective cultural identity can be. All those years of believing I had Irish lineage made the past St. Patrick's Day a very strange experience. For the past sixty plus years, I have spent the weeks before March 17 selecting the right shades of green for my clothing, the proper accessories/jewelry, and even the perfect nail polish color. This year felt so strange because all that planning felt hollow because it was just about surface appearance; I felt like a poser after all. I knew all that green did not reflect the reality of my ancestors. Interesting, is it not that even though I did not know who my ancestors were, I wanted to wear clothing that identified with them? How important is that connection?

Joining DAR and GSMD was transformational for me because I now had names (the colonel) and behaviors (the *Mayflower*) to associate with my ancestry. *But* I am not sure, after all this writing, that I can clearly articulate why this is true. Belonging to both organizations marks the first time in my life that I was associating with others based on my ancestry, and I was representing them in the group. At GSMD meetings, attendance is taken by the name of William Brewster, and at DAR meetings I wear a pin with the name of Colonel Timothy Paige on it. I cannot fully describe how that makes me feel, but it is quite spectacular.

In addition, all this genealogical discovery has had an unanticipated benefit within my immediate family. I will share a part of an email I received from my brother Bob, a Protestant minister (that story is another book), regarding his feelings about William Brewster and knowing he is an ancestor.

> I am so intrigued by what you have uncovered concerning our family. Thanks for the amazing work you have tirelessly put into this. I have read many documents connected to the Brewster's and the more I read the more I am

stirred deeply concerning who I and my family are. (Personal Communication; June 7, 2017)

I could barely read this email because those darn onions made me cry. The kind word from my brother were wonderful on so many levels. Beyond the personal validation of my research, he was articulating exactly what I am trying to reveal in this paragraph. Now, maybe, if our ancestor was Jack the Ripper, the feelings would be different. However, as I type this, I begin to realize that the discovery of the colonel and William Brewster was just icing on the cake.

Emma was not a notorious serial killer, but she certainly offered a contrast to other family members. Emma's history was not as elevated as the colonel and William Brewster. In her case, I began to surmise that getting her record and memory untangled was important to her, and it became important to me. Emma was the onion in the whole family stew. (So was my mother if you think about it—a Catholic onion at that.) As I have recorded my discoveries in this memoir, it was the cigar box and the dream of Emma that propelled me into this endeavor. It was in the cigar box I found the birth certificate of Aunt Anne and realized my grandmother's name was *not* Emma Nancy O'Hara. However, Emma kind of dropped to the sidelines as I got all obsessed with DAR and GSMD.

In retrospect, I see that my revelations about Emma were (1) the most startling, (2) the most frequent, and (3) and the real catalyst for all the other discoveries. My first breakthrough came with Nancy, and she wrote me because of the connection of Emma to Aunt Edna/Ruth. Nancy provided me a wealth of newspaper information about Emma. I was proud of the colonel, but it was for Emma I felt not just pride but also compassion and sorrow. I visualized her youth and her growing up in Harrisburg in the right social circles. I imagined her musical talent and how her artistic gifts were appreciated by family, friends, and her church. Then by her death in 1929, everyone, including my father, is trying, either intentionally or because they were misled, to expunge her memory.

Can you imagine having a family that tried to obliterate your existence? Her name was not included in her parents' obituaries. Aunt

Anne's death certificate listed her mother as unknown. For whatever reason, Emma's birth certificate is nowhere to be found. Her firstborn is known as her brother, not as her son. Her second-born was adopted away after a year never to know her mother. Emma's pain did not end there however. Her first husband was insane, and her third child, Helen, died from the effects of syphilis. She married Pappy, and my dad nearly died from spinal meningitis. Her sixth child, John, was stillborn, and she was not yet forty years old. I do not need a time machine to surmise that the mental health support, especially for women, was not too accessible in 1929.

What was it like to be in a family with a son you could never acknowledge? Emma's immediate family seemed to feel that eliminating her memory was the best way to deal with the embarrassment of her choices. I have made some dreadful personal choices in my life, and the temptation to ignore and obstruct is very strong. I believe her first husband was a family-engineered attempt to marry her off and move back to social acceptability in Harrisburg. Too bad the family was not more selective about the man because he simply took her into deeper sorrow and suffering. Once she was in Philadelphia with Pappy, she was no longer around to remind them of the scandals. When she died, the funeral was quick, and now Emma was out of sight and out of mind.

I suddenly realized that trend began to reverse when I took the first step and made a public declaration of her family connections on an online family tree. That was how Nancy found me, and I found out about Aunt Edna/Ruth, and that was recorded here. Now if this memoir is published, all of my readers will know Emma's story, and memory of her will be restored. All this time, I was thinking of this memoir as my story, and now I know it is really Emma's. How can a family be together when an important link is missing?

There is a connection between this earthly existence and the next heavenly life. I began this memoir by writing, in the most plain and straightforward way that I could, that I am not a spiritualist. I do not go to mediums, séances, or try to contact the spirit realm. *The Catechism of the Catholic Church* (2115, 2116, 2117) is very clear about the church's stance on using divination and magic to learn about the future, consult the dead, and/or tame occult powers. And in faith, I accept and adhere to this doctrine.

The communion of saints, the body of Christ, is made up of all the saints on earth (the church militant), in Purgatory (the church pertinent), and in Heaven (the church triumphant, and therefore, there is communion *among holy persons* and *in holy things* (CCC 948). In this memoir, I have described the gratitude I felt at Masses, the supervision of my hash brown preparation, and the promptings to press forward in my genealogical search. I never sought any of this, and I think that is the important distinction here. The forbidden act is to openly seek this experience through human measures whereas the accepted path is to receive graces and insights given to us as God's unmerited favor.

I now marvel at Emma's humility. She lets me discover her part of this story on my own. She did not come as a vengeful spirit like Fruma Sarah in *Fiddler on the Roof*. Unlike me, she neither spilled a torrent of words nor indicated that she wanted me to clear her name. Her concern was to bring the family together, and then she allowed me to discover what that meant. She might have felt some responsibility for the splintering of the family, but I feel there is very little of that here. I believe her focus was that it was better for all of us to know who we are and where we came from. She wanted to remind us that we all have a great cloud of witnesses who are interested and watching to both see how we use the onions in our life and to cheer us on to the end because they are waiting at the ultimate finish line.

My brother clearly indicated that was happening for him. My son is delighted by the colonel and William Brewster, but he is thrilled by the discovered Jewish heritage. If you have been paying attention, you know exactly how I feel about all of this. It is like one cell in a living body that has a purpose, but its proper functioning can only be considered in the context of the health of the whole body. I believe Emma knows that in the greater scheme of life, her personal interests are secondary. However, when you stand back and look at the whole picture, you can see how the destruction of Emma's spirit and life had a domino effect on those who came after her. We completely lost who we were and where we came from. We could not draw on the strength of the colonel and Willian Brewster because they were obliterated by two generations of compounded tragedy. Emma's story led us back to our heritage.

Discovering this heritage does not mean my life is going to get easier. There is no magic formula to eliminate all suffering and difficulty in this life. Eliminate all the onions and think of what is lost in cookery. So many individuals long to hear the strains of "We Are the Champions" (or *Pomp and Circumstances*, *Here Comes the Bride*—fill in the appropriate soundtrack) in their lives. There might be a ring, a cup, a trophy, or a diploma to commemorate the event, but the triumph lasts only for a moment and does not guarantee a life of joy and happiness.

The list of individuals who once experienced a human championship and then experienced despair, disgrace, and/or poverty is long. On the other side, the moment Jesus uttered the words, "It is finished," He was the most powerful human being ever to inhabit the planet. He made it to the finish line, and He spent all He had to get there. Yet He died on a tree (a curse), and He was so brutalized He was barely recognizable as human, but he was a champion. Can you imagine who was waiting for Him at the finish line? Better yet, if you make the right life choices, it can be Jesus and your clan waiting for you.

Oh, one last bit of information you should know about before I end my memoir. Because of continued research, I have found, including the colonel and the captain, that I have seven—dare I say the Magnificent Seven—great grandfathers who were revolutionary patriots. Also, my Jeep Patriot is the darling of my DAR sisters.

Chapter 29

WE ARE FAMILY

> Everyone can see we're together as we walk on by
> (And) And we fly just like birds of a feather
> I won't tell no lie
> All of the people around us they say (they say)
> Can they be that close (that's right)
> Just let me say for the record
> We're giving love as a family does.
> (Nile Rodgers and Bernard Edwards [1979], We
> Are Family)

Using this lyric for this chapter has a deeper meaning than just matching the lyrics to the story I tell. In looking for the authors names to attribute the lyrics, I found an interesting story in Wikipedia.com. The authors had their own act, chic, but their producer wanted them to write lyrics for other big acts. The authors did not want their lyrics to get lost in such bigger-than-life performers like the Rolling Stones; no one would know who wrote the piece because the focus is Mic, Keith, and the boys. The lyrics easily evolved and focused on Sister Sledge and her sisters. The authors went into the studio where that famous melody emerged. Now the song means so much more than the love between sisters and has become an anthem for family unity. My point is, sometimes, great literature and great music emerge in much unexpected ways. One other thing you might find interesting is that I now know I have seven DAR eligible ancestors in the colonel's line.

As I have had time to ponder all these events and individuals, my imagination kind of ran away with me, and I visualized/heard a family discussion session in the (Paige) Cloud. The Paige participants were William Brewster, Nathaniel Paige, his son Christopher, his grandson, the colonel, his great grandson, the captain, his son Martin, his son Timothy, his son George, his son Pappy, and his son Dad (I have my own list of begets here). The setting is the family's the (Paige) Cloud, and my men are enjoying some fellowship and a boys' night out.

Colonel said, "It is interesting to see what is going on with the family these days. It is sad however that they seem so splintered and all over the place. They are not in contact with one another. They will have a surprise when they get here and meet so many strangers let alone seeing so many unfamiliar faces. I suspect, William, you will be a big surprise."

Captain said, "Father, you had nine children, and five of us were boys, so you should expect to see these folks all over the place."

Nathaniel said, "Great-great-Grandson, we established the Paige name in the beginning of the United States, though not as early as Brewster, I will admit. You, my son and grandsons, were active members in the rebellion and then involved in the establishing of the country. We have a proud heritage."

William said, "Thank you for your acknowledgment, Nathaniel. When I arrived in 1620, the USA was a little more than a savage and hostile outpost that all but guaranteed an early grave; that is if you survived crossing the ocean to get there. By the time you came along, the place was a paradise."

Colonel said, "The country is so large now. We were together in Vermont, Massachusetts, and New Hampshire, and now they live in California—wherever that is—almost three thousand miles away. Of course, the Daughters of the American Revolution are helpful because it reminds our female family members where they come from, but still, it seems like we have lost track of some of the family.

Frank? (three voices answer, 'Yes?') You, Frank Albert, your family had wandered away from any contact for a long time."

Christopher said, "Yes, but let us not forget his daughter-in-law is a Catholic—a Paige who is a Papist, unbelievable! It seems Frank Jr. was sending a message to the family with that one. I think he redeemed himself somewhat however because Irene was a soldier and an officer at that."

Nathaniel said, "Yes, Son, I would certainly say the Catholic line was somewhat problematic. Of course, by the time we became aware, we were in no position to protest, forgive the pun. In addition, our Catholic attitudes have altered since stepping into this reality. Gradually, as the prayers broke through all I could feel was gratitude, and lo and behold, it was that marriage that ultimately brought grace to us all."

Frank Jr. said, "I admit I knew that Irene would outrage the family, *but* I felt I was not good enough—never measured up to expectations, so at the time, I felt, why not? Besides, she was a beautiful blond. I converted to Catholicism for her too, and that is when things began to change."

Pappy said, "I take responsibility for that, Son; life has so much clarity from here. I lost my mother young, and then my wife and your mother and two baby boys, John and George, and it just seemed like more than I could deal with. When Emma and George died, everyone was blaming everyone else because the hurt was so deep. Your grandparents, Lysel and John, blamed me for it all. Moreover, you almost died with the spinal meningitis, and I had nothing left in me. I just thought you needed a mother, and Mom Rawlings seemed to be the perfect solution."

Frank Jr. said, "Now I understand, Dad. You were just doing what you could during a terrible time. God knows I struggled in my role as a father, so I can no longer judge you. Dad, you were the one who disappeared though. I will never forget the day of your funeral. I thought I would feel relief when you finally died, but I was devastated. In spite of my ambivalence, I was still burying my father, so I was sad, but on the other hand, we had so many negative words between us; I was a mess."

Pappy said, "Well, Son, my mother, Louisa, died when I was barely one year old, and your Grandpa George had his hands full as well, so off I went to other family members to be raised. I guess the wanderlust just took root, and I was all over the place. You know, Son, the family was none too happy when you married Irene."

Frank Jr. said, "That was my point after all, but the good part was that Catholics pray for us after we die, unlike our other Protestant relatives. Besides, one of the reasons I made the cut here is because I converted to marry her. Thank God for Lourdes; my experience there literally saved my soul. I went there drunk as a skunk thinking I would get some of the healing water for Suzy's polio. It turned out I had a real encounter with God, sobered me right up. It would be nice if I could say I was a different person, but life is not that easy, simple but not easy, but in spite of myself, I made it here."

Both Nathaniel and Christopher said, "Imagine how we felt."

William: Yes indeed. What a surprise to find out direct access to Heaven took more than faith and the Bible. Did Martin Luther make it?

Nathaniel said, "Not sure, but he will spend much more time "cleaning up" before he does."

William said, "Though I have no love for the pope, I saw what happened to those Catholics in England after King Henry decided to make himself pope. He tortured and murdered men, women, and children and gave the church property to his friends. When he was done with them, he turned on us, so I had some more sympathy than you did, but who knew they had it right?"

Pappy said, "Of course, Irene was not much interested in us; she thought Emma's name was Nancy O'Hara! We are not Irish."

Frank Jr. said, "That was part of the backstory I told because the real story hurt too much. I thought if I could make them forget you and there would be no memory of you, I could pay you back. You should be happy because my son Robert Allen is a Protestant and a minister like the three of you (William, Christopher, and Nathaniel)."

Christopher said, "I guess we can be. As difficult as it is to admit, the prayers and graces from your daughter's prayers are lovely."

Nathaniel said, "In her prayers, she makes sure to remind me that those graces are coming from a Catholic. I might add, there is a bit of you in her Frank."

William said, "She is particularly pointed with me, it seems."

Frank Jr said, "She is a Paige after all."

Colonel said, "So how is the plan going?"

Timothy said, "We sent Emma to bring the message of reuniting the family to her; she got the full, 'You will never forget this dream' treatment. You were right about simple but direct working best. If she had any idea what we planned for her, she would have rolled over in bed and written the whole thing off to a bad meal."

George said, "Of course, time is not measured here like it is on earth, so what seems like only a moment here is years and decades there. She did seem to have problems getting a good husband. You know, Frank, part of that was the crazy marriage problems alcohol created for you. Then on top of it all, she had her polio."

Frank Jr said, "I know, Grandad, it was the *Days of Wine and Roses* all over again. As hard as it was to believe at first, it was part of the plan to make her strong enough to persist beyond all the difficulties she would encounter."

Colonel said, "She loves the DAR part. It is so funny because she thought she was finally to the end of the family quest the day she went to Pappy's grave. It was not easy to keep her going. She had so much going on in her life, but once she got to the DAR, she was going on her own steam. Now she knows there is more DAR ancestry there than she ever dreamed possible, way more, thirteen to be exact."

William said, "I was a big surprise to her too."

Colonel said, "The DAR seemed to be the motivation she needed to spend the money—she gets that from you Frank—and dig into the family. Little did she know what else we were planning."

George said, "We almost lost her at one point. My great granddaughter posted a timeline showing that I only had one son, George Jr. and that Louisa and I were married many years. It hit her hard, and she was ready to quit, and she is not much on quitting. It lets you know the depth of her discouragement."

Timothy said, "Don't we know it? We all watched her bull her way through a PhD. She had some nasty stuff thrown her way—especially by the department chair—but she just kept 'one day at a time' in her head. Even the AA stuff worked to her benefit."

Frank Jr. said, "Yes, she got that from going to AA meetings with me. Did I tell you about the term paper she wrote in college because a professor bad-mouthed AA?"

Pappy said, "Yes, Frank, you have, and remember, this is eternity. You know she calls me Pappy! She said prayers to comfort me in my last moments before death and brought flowers to my grave, and now I watch her make hash brown potatoes."

George said, "Well, now I am Great-Grandfather George to her. She sure took on my great granddaughter to show her that they lost track of my second son Frank. Then there was confusion because they thought you were Frank Hill Paige, but he was just another cousin in the Paige clan. Good thing Tim remembered you existed. Do you know she turned in the DAR paperwork?"

All (in unison) said, "Do we!"

William said, "She did not wait to tackle the GSMD either."

Martin said, "She was praying all the time for our help, especially when she thought George and Louisa were lost to her. She went clean back to Nathaniel in those prayers."

William said, "She did not know about me yet."

Timothy said, "I know she was constantly saying that if she could trace the family line to Rebecca and me, she was home free, and she finally broke through. She has become a pretty good detective."

Martin said, "She even found a line in the DAR through Captain then me and then Timothy and his daughter Martha, so that will make the process even easier."

Colonel said, "You do know she is writing about this whole experience. I have noticed that she writes because it helps her sort things out. I chuckled when I read her first chapter because I knew she thought her ancestry search was all over."

Christopher said, "She knows better now."

William said, "She sure does."

Captain said, "Yes indeed, and she keeps writing without a clear notion where we are leading her, but now, she cannot stop herself. The plan is working well. Do you think she will get it published?"

William said "If stubborn counts then I say yes."

Martin said, "Are we agreed where this journey is going to take her?"

Nathaniel said, "Well? (minutes of silence pass)."

Colonel said, "You know there is an unanticipated turn in her story?"

Captain said, "Yes, I heard she was so excited about learning about us that she thought Irene's family should get some attention."

Martin said, "Yes, she does not seem to do 'downtime' really well. She even checked her DNA, whatever that is exactly. I am still in awe of the world in which she resides. The Jewish heritage she always suspected is now a reality. Can you imagine the heritage that she carries? She is descended from *Mayflower* passengers (William), ministers and deacons (Nathaniel, Christopher) from both the Pilgrims and Methodists, governors and lawyers, seven Revolutionary War veterans (including the colonel and the captain), Catholic, and now a Jewish heritage."

Timothy said, "Well, the ultimate end is to be reunited with us, and I understand she plans on having a dance with us all. She loved to dance, but these days, the polio has temporarily postponed her dancing days."

George said, "So I heard she plans on shedding the crutches and waltzing a good piece of eternity away."

Pappy said, "What a joy it will be to meet her face-to-face; I feel I know her so well. She loves hash brown potatoes, and as a cook, I am very interested in her frying techniques. She talks to me as she fixes them; she seems to know I am watching. The Masses she has for me bring such peace to my soul because I know I am not forgotten back on earth. I now see all the brokenness and loss, including Frank's physical ailments and her polio, all combined into wonder and great joy for me."

Frank Jr. said, "You guys are all getting in line behind me. My little girl and I have some things to say to one another. I died so suddenly, and there were cross words between us over her second husband. Just before Irene passed, I stopped by her hospital room. When Irene told her I had been there, she was so disappointed that her mother saw me, and Irene did not seem to care one way or the other. She never questioned the veracity of the story; all she could say is, 'You saw Dad?' She wanted every detail: 'How did he look?' 'What was he wearing?' 'Where was he?' 'Did he say anything?' I could see the heartache in her eyes. All she got from Irene were one word disinterested answers. Of course, Irene was loaded with pain meds; that was how she could see me. Suzy is still waiting to see me herself, so after she gets through the heavenly customs process, I plan on being there at the front of the line and have the first dance with her. Did I tell you guys about the term paper?"

Chapter 30

EPILOGUE: RHYTHM OF THE RAIN

> Listen to the rhythm of the falling rain
> Telling me just what a fool I've been
> I wish that it would go and let me cry in vain
> And let me be alone again
> Now the only girl I've ever loved has gone away
> Looking for a brand-new start
> Little does she know that when she left that day
> Along with her she took my heart

This lyric is a golden oldie from my "tween" years. I heard it one day as I was driving along and thinking about all my genealogical adventures. The music and lyrics come from John Gummoe of the Cascades, and they recorded it in 1962. I think it is interesting that the original band began with US Navy personnel. I like synchronicity, as you may well know by now, so the military connection feels right to me. By the way, it was *not* raining while I was pondering. It just occurred to me that I loved this music, and it should be part of my soundtrack, but I was done writing, right?

So you would not think I added this lyric just to include a favorite song, I should comment on its relevance. On the surface, the lyric points to a lost love (*eros*), but I can relate it to the loss of family (*philio*) relationships. I must be honest that I was not looking for a brand-new start, as the lyrics suggest, but I had one. All the experiences I write about in this memoir have had a profound impact on my life.

The precise moment that the trajectory changed was the summer day in 1977 that I came in possession of Pappy's cigar box. I had that box in my possession for about fifteen years before I had "the dream" of Emma. It was another ten years until I received the letter from Mount Moriah Cemetery confirming that Pappy was buried there. (Finding this location to even make the inquiry was, shall I say, luck?) Another ten years passed before I made the trip to Philadelphia and to discover that the site of Pappy's grave was situated in the spot that Emma was standing in my dream, over twenty years before.

I saw Emma in that dream, and I knew her name because the cigar box birth certificate of Aunt Anne named Emma as her mother. I did not love her, and I did not know anything about her, but I knew her name. As time went on, the onions of life brought tears, and an occasional cranial detonation, as I unraveled the secrecy, the denial, and the tragedy that surrounded her memory. I came to see that the real success in this life was really a measure of how we are remembered after we have passed from it—like William Brewster and the colonel.

The irony was that looking into Emma and her family was an afterthought as I awaited approval of my membership in the Daughters of the American Revolution (DAR) and the General Society of Mayflower Descendants (GSMD). I was just filling time when more details about Emma's life emerged. I soon came to see the story of Emma's life, up to that point, was like the falling rain trying to wash away her memory and pretend she did not exist. As I made quite clear in my introduction, I had absolutely no idea (a) where this story was going, (b) that Emma was the reason for much of it, and (c) that writing everything down was essential.

Nancy's email was also important in the additional discoveries about Emma. I received her initial email asking if the Emma I had in my online family tree could be the same Emma who was the mother of her adopted Aunt Edna. The moment I read her email, I knew they were one and the same person. She sent me a picture of Aunt

Edna/Ruth, as we came to call her, and there was the "lazy eye" that both Dad and my brother Bob have. In addition, they had, even though never meeting, very similar likes and interests.

Nancy provided all the newspaper articles about Emma's social status and her musical abilities as a young girl playing at both church and social events. Emma had promise and a prominent societal standing. More newspaper clippings showed a hasty marriage, the birth of a short-lived child, an ex-husband declared insane, and divorce. Finally, Nancy sent the very sad obituaries of both Emma's parents that omitted the detail that either one of them had a daughter named Emma. Emma died on the sixteenth of January in Philadelphia, had a coroner's inquest on the seventeenth, and was buried one hundred miles away on the eighteenth. Once she was in the ground, she was washed away by the snow and rain.

Emma changed my life, and I came to love (*philos*) her. So here I am again yet again at the keyboard. I do know this writing has to stop at some point, but as we all know, life does not stop happening, and new developments do crop up. Maybe calling this an epilogue will help to finally reach a conclusion. So what is new since I last wrote?

I am fully ensconced in both the DAR and the GSMD. In the DAR, I am now the vice-regent in my chapter. Who could foresee such a meteoric rise in such a short time? In a year, I would be the regent of my chapter unless God has other plans for me. I still love the meetings, and my eyes mist every time I recite, "Yea, I have a goodly heritage" when we conduct the opening ritual for the DAR meetings. God did have other plans for me, however, because I am still with DAR, but I now (a) live in Florida (and yet another coincidence because I moved on August 20—Emma's birthday), (b) retired after twenty-six years of teaching in higher education, and (c) I have discovered thirteen DAR patriots from both the Paige [10] and Emma's family [3] for the total [13]! How do you like that?

In 2020, I did a presentation for my DAR chapter on "Women in the Military," and yes, of course, my mother was the centerpiece—complete with a picture of her in her first lieutenant's army uniform. I also spoke about my hopes for a military career until my dad told me polio would prevent this from happening. Of more interest is how this came about. During the previous summer, when we were doing the planning for the chapter yearbook, the topic of women in the military was suggested as a topic for a chapter presentation. I was sitting in my chair waiting to see who would select this topic. Then it happened.

The best description I can give it would be to call it a spiritual kick in the butt: "This is for you!" So I spoke up with a tepid, "I will do this." It was only after I said yes to the topic that I suddenly realized I had plenty of information on this topic, and why had I even hesitated? I had so many ideas for the presentation that I worked on it the next day, and so it was done eight months before I presented it. My presentation was well received by the way. I still marvel at my disinterest when the topic was suggested. So you see, left to our own devices, we have the potential to miss some of our best opportunities. In 2021, I presented on William Brewster and the four hundredth anniversary of the *Mayflower* landing.

I have attended annual meetings of the GSMD. At the second meeting, I was accompanied by my son Jimmie and his oldest son, Brayden. They were both interested in their Mayflower ancestors, so I got them memberships for their birthdays. Brayden, at eleven years of age, was the youngest person in the room, by far, and he loved every minute of it. He was turning into quite a historian, and in particular, he was fascinated by World War I. Truth be told, he got this interest from the video game *Battlefield*, and I was astonished by the depth of his knowledge on this topic. In addition, my son is as engrossed by data about our ancestors as I am. I cannot tell you how delighted I was to have both at the meeting with me—another unintended consequence of my journey into genealogy. Now, I belong to a Florida chapter, and I have been able to attend meetings via Zoom.

My brother Bob and I visited for the first time in many years in 2018. Much of our conversation was focused on the genealogical data I had collected. He is particularly interested in William Brewster. This is no surprise to me because he is a minister as well and is quite proud to be a descendant of William Brewster, not to mention deacons Nathaniel Paige and his son Christopher. I was able to share the data I had collected to verify that they were indeed our ancestor. (So interesting that these latter two Paige men spent years ministering in and around the Mohawk Valley in New York where Bob lived for over twenty years.) Bob was very grateful for the research and my dogged persistence in getting to the bottom of the Paige family history. Emma wanted me to bring the family together, and I had no idea it would impact my immediate family so much. Now Bob and I live in Florida, and I spent 2020 and 2021 Thanksgiving dinner at his table with my niece and nephew retelling our family story of the famous feast in Plymouth.

I am very relieved that I wrote all my experiences down, on paper, as they were happening. I find myself now getting all tangled up in my web of narrative and chronology. Quite a few persons have commented that this story should be written, and I tell them I have thirty chapters. I am hoping that now that this story is on paper, I can give it to family and friends so they can understand my journey. Just think this might be coming to a website near you in a very short time.

Remember chapter 21 with the tangled spider web and my exploding head? In that chapter, I recounted my discovery that Emma's brother Kenneth was really her son—her firstborn child. I have made contact with my first cousin, the daughter of Kenneth, Peggy. I saw a common entry for Emma on another family tree online. I had been waiting two years for someone to show up indicating a familial connection with Emma's family because my searches had been futile. I sent an email to the owner of the family tree and waited for a response. In about ten days, I was contacted by a female, and she told me she had just discovered that her aunt was really her grandmother. Can you hear the exploding heads?

Because she is Kenneth's daughter, I announced to her I was her first cousin because our fathers were half-brothers. I felt a shift in the ectoplasm, and she responded she was "flabbergasted…Did you know Emma had other siblings? I did know them, and they all kept this very hush-hush." Yes, as a matter of fact, I know this very well. She should meet the reluctant bureaucrat in Pennsylvania who was no help to me in locating Emma's birth certificate.

My genealogy experience has shown me that a newly discovered family needs time to be digested. Marsha in California, whose grandfather was Pappy's brother, took some time to wrap her head around me as a new family tie. Perhaps she thought I would fly there with a camera crew to film our family reunion for my social media site (that I do not have). In my case, I know I am missing a whole lot of relatives. I felt the need to include Nancy in my online conversations because both she and Peggy are connected to Emma. Nancy is niece to Edna/Ruth and Peggy the daughter of Kenneth. It suddenly occurred to me that I was bringing the family together yet again.

This new family connection prompted me to once again investigate the man who was Uncle Kenneth's birth father. Emma and Joseph seem to be just two young star-crossed teens who went too far. However, for a moment, I got tangled up in birth dates, and I thought Joseph was nine years older than Emma; he was eight months younger. Suddenly, I had visions of seduction and a predator taking advantage. Emma was brought up in the church. She traveled in an upper middle class and Gentile milieu and played the piano at church and social functions. Now even though I know the age difference for what it is, this does not preclude some of this type of behavior going on, on either side. My other question is why did they not just marry? Did one of the families see the match as below their social status? The paternity of Aunt Edna/Ruth was finally solved by Nancy when her birth certificate showed up after years of searching. Edna/Ruth's father was Charles, a salesman from New York, who left no digital footprints to follow.

I always believed Emma was coerced into marriage with Charles. The family needed a way to move forward from these two pregnancies, and this marriage was arranged to safely tuck her away and move beyond her scandalous past. Only Charles had syphilis that not only took the life of her third child, whose middle name is Emma, but also made him insane. I believe once Emma realized she was *ruined*, combined with the scorn she experienced from the rest of the family and society, only then came her, "What the hell!" attitude.

My true confession here is I have had three husbands (between 1968 and 1992). I was going through my third divorce when the dream about Emma came. (I put these two events together as I was reflecting on all this.) The more I learn about Emma, the more I think I know why I was the choice for her nocturnal visit to bring the family together. I have had a personal life that included being pregnant before I was married. I married, divorced, and remarried within five years. As I told my brother Bob I had three husbands, so who can better understand Emma's tumultuous life—and three husbands make for lots of tumult!—than me, her wayward granddaughter.

I do not say this to make light of the events in my life or with any self-pity. I made decisions that have made me the person I am today, but some of them were very bad. I heard a very powerful statement recently, "Every choice you make changes you." and I would add either for good or for bad. This is where being a Catholic is my salvation. I have access to the sacramental benefits of recollection and a patron saint in Mary Magdalene who helps me move past my past. I would never want to do these things again, *but* I believe what does not kill you makes you stronger. I understand how Emma was overwhelmed and misunderstood. I lived through the divorce culture of the 1960 and '70s, and still, my guilt is oppressive at times. I can only imagine what Emma felt because one's virtue could be easily lost in the early 1900s.

Finally, I decided to try and publish this memoir. So if you are reading this, it means (a) I was able to tell Emma's story, and (b) I successfully meandered my way through the publishing maze (or found enough money to self-publish).

Hopefully, this is my real final thought because all good things must come to an end. When you hear the rhythm of the falling rain, think of Emma's story and remember the words of the famous bard from Stratford-on-Avon. "The quality of mercy is not strained; it droppeth as the gentle rain from Heaven upon the place beneath" (William Shakespeare, *The Merchant of Venice*).

Look what Nancy found! I finished these thoughts as I include her photos. The symmetry is perfect. I began this memoir pondering in a cemetery, and we will end there. Can you believe it is raining outside?

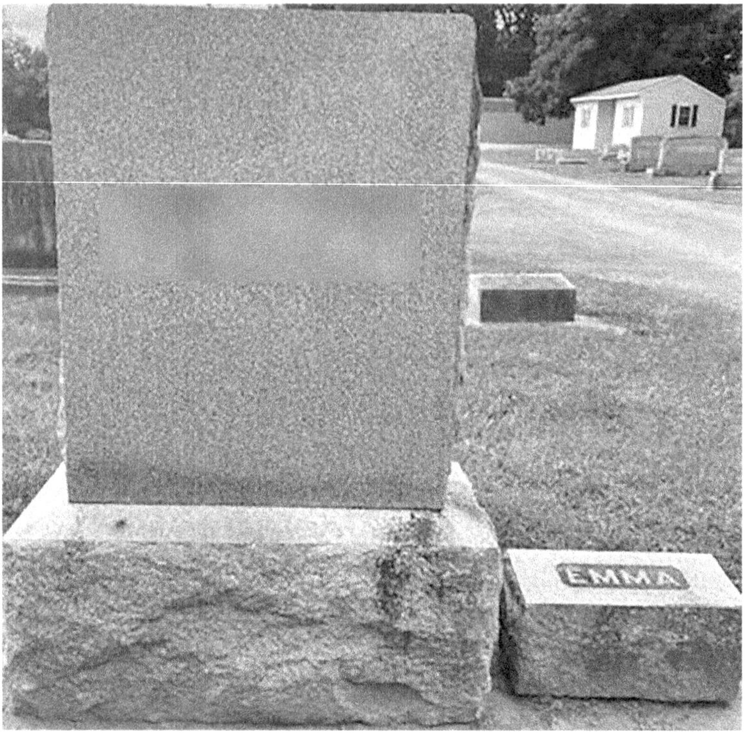
EMMA

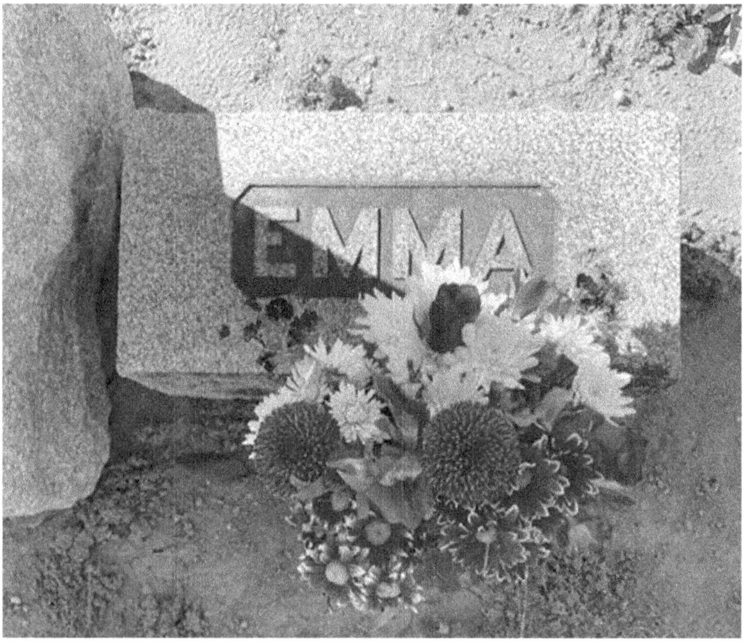
EMMA

This memoir was initiated. so many years ago, while I pondered my Paige genealogy at the same time I was tending family graves on a Memorial Day weekend. It seems this memoire will end the same way. On Memorial Day weekend 2022 I was pondering a photograph, that has hung on my wall for more than a decade. It is a bridal picture of me on May 11, 1975, the day I married Jimmie and Amanda's father. After all these years I suddenly focused on the bridal gown I was wearing (and that I picked out) and I had a stunning insight. The gown is the exact dress that Emma wore in my dream (without veil and flowers of course). Read my description in my earlier chapters and my NDE clarity of that scene. Some might say the Emma in my dream was an unconscious manifestation of some inner angst. I know better. Cue in "The Way We Were" and check out the dress.

Paige Genealogy Names with * and italics indicate DAR eligible ancestors. Yellow highlight traces Brewster family line.

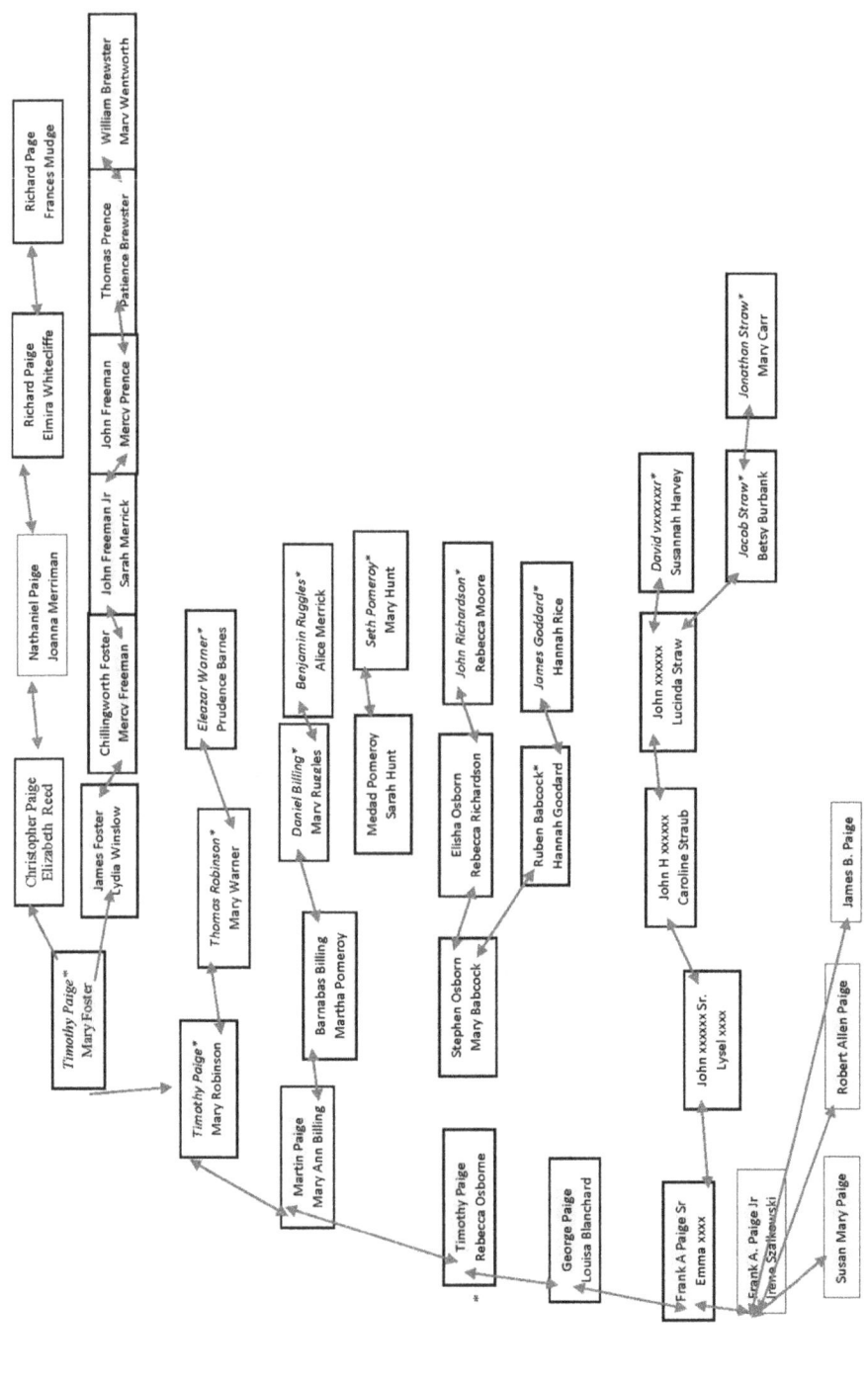

200

About the Author

Susan Mary Paige (Suzy to family and friends) is a recently retired baby boomer. She was born in an army hospital to parents who both served in the military. Polio complicated but did not deter the course of her life except for the military career she thought she was destined to follow. Instead, she earned three college degrees and had a working career in both the public and private sectors that included twenty-six years of teaching in higher education.

Genealogy came as an interest, later in her life, after her three children were grown and married. It turned just about everything she thought she knew about her family on its head.